To Lesley,

Thank for buying my
proud of the 'e

ed Vanson

Brilliantly
Bonkers

by

Ed Vanson

New Generation Publishing

THE PROLOGUE

I had a hangover. Not just a small inconvenient one, oh no, this was a whopper and it seemed to have spread to my entire body which was odd. I had never had an all-encompassing hangover before but here I was, cramp-ridden and sore, in my parents' spare bedroom. Everything seemed to hurt, right down to having blistered feet. Can alcohol do that? Surely not but it seemed to have done. Resisting the urge to throw my alarm clock across the room I sat up, rubbed my eyes and took it all in. The day before had been quite a day you see, one of the biggest days in the nation's sporting calendar. It had been the Virgin London Marathon.

My head was still throbbing.

I was never really sure if this would be a story worth telling but, as what you are about to read progressed in normal time back in 2012 and then 2013, it became apparent that it was quite a journey, in both the physical and emotional sense. I started making notes here and notes there and suddenly I had loads of paper with notes on them and the making of a tale covering the adventure so I thought 'what the heck', I may as well write it. It had been a fine time, an exciting time and a time I really enjoyed. So let's get cracking: I feel like I need a narrator for this bit but I haven't got one so you will have to imagine my voice. Or if you don't know me and don't know what I sound like, you can feel free to imagine the next bit being spoken in a voice of your choosing. Or if you do know me and know what I sound like and, as I do, think that I really don't have a future on the radio or as a narrator, just imagine someone else.

As with all good stories I should start by filling you in on a little background information and so, if you are ready and sitting comfortable, (or standing, or lying down, there are no rules on how to read so far as I am aware) I shall do so.

It all starts with a birth of a fat baby early one October morning, in a London hospital, the realisation of two people's parental dreams. Those two people were and are my parents and that fat baby was and is me, all nine pounds eight ounces of me, then I mean, not now, I weigh a fair bit more than that these days. This baby was called Edward Henry Vanson and he joined a tight family, the sort of family that apparently drank London dry when he made his earth debut. Although probably not Mum, I imagine she wasn't totally up for a beer at that point in time. It was a happy time for me, I am sure, as I got to stretch my legs after spending nine months somewhat short on space and being a bit cooped up. This is the story of one of that baby's adventures, the result of what some people still refer to as "another silly idea".

Alas I have to start with a bit of a sad story. I don't want to upset you but it is important to the story you have just picked up. It is a story concerning someone that became quite a powerful influence on all this: In 1978 Grandma Vanson died of heart disease. I was only just over a year old and the only grandchild she ever met. I believe that I have vague memories of her and probably don't realistically, but I have always felt as though I knew her and I am told that we spent a lot of time together. Apparently Mum used to wheel me over in my pram to see her at least once a week and we were good mates. Dad has always spoken of her and there were photos of her on the wall when we were kids. As a result we three kids all asked questions, which were always answered so she has always been present in our family really, in every way – bar in a physical sense.

When I was a young lad, I got into watching the London Marathon on television and I was fascinated by the crowds, the noise, the pure effort, the winners, the losers and the fundraisers. Some of them were in fancy dress which, to my young mind, was brilliant. Imagine running a marathon in fancy dress! I saw people had the names of people they were running for on their T-shirts and also mentioned them at roadside television interviews. That made quite an impression on me and I remarked to Dad that "one day I'll run the London Marathon for Grandma" which I can only assume was an unplanned statement and a sentence used by the people I was watching on the television. "Good idea," said Dad, supportive as ever: "You could run for the British Heart Foundation." I agreed.

It was a conversation that Dad probably thought a nice but forgettable chat with his young son. After all, kids say silly things. I had already announced in previous times that I was going to win the World Cup for England after all. Quite rightly, he probably thought I would soon forget what I had just said and get on with my life, a typical dreaming child.

I never did win the World Cup with England[1] but I never did forget that conversation.

---

[1] I refuse to totally believe that dream is over by the way. Never say never and all that. I am only in my late 30s so plenty of time yet.

MANY, MANY YEARS LATER

In early 2012, I was recovering from both an emergency abdominal surgery following a nasty insect bite and then an operation to have my left big toe fused following a road traffic accident in 2008 where I got hit by a car as I cycled home. One of my injuries that night was a smashed big toe, which the collision had managed to break in no less than seven places and so needed surgery. I had had metal and pins inserted then but over the last couple of years arthritis had set in and the toe had become more and more painful so the appointment was made and I had to have it fused, which means that the joint was taken out, along with the metal and pins previously inserted and then a big metal bar was put in instead, which means that the toe can no longer bend but should ideally sort it all out once and for all. To top off this fun little episode in my life I then became sick with an MRSA infection and faced surgery to sort both that and then again to sort my toe as I couldn't make it sit down. Whilst I had been in hospital after my collision with that very silly driver, a man died in a bed near me which shook me as I listened to it all but it also rather galvanised me to a degree: I would get back to sport and I would live life to the full. This whole accident experience had scared me a little. Not because I was ever close to death and nor was I ever critically ill. Let me be clear, that was never the case. When I say it scared me, I mean in that it *could* have been that serious, if I had landed awkwardly as I fell off the car or if a car had been coming the other way as I lay in the road immediately after the impact for example. I started to feel very lucky indeed. I realised that I had to grab life, live it, love it, achieve within it. More than anything I wanted to achieve something, something big, something massive and something that would prove I am still here.

I was given some bad news after my toe fusion which knocked me back quite a bit – my surgeon told me that it was his opinion that I would probably not run another marathon or play football again as my toe wouldn't be able to take it. Two of my biggest passions had seemingly been taken from me, although a lot of people that had seen me attempt to play football would argue that I had never been able to "play" anyway but that is another story and I was devastated for a short while nonetheless. To paint the picture I was off work, bored, sore, on crutches and really quite blue. In short I was pretty grumpy. A short period of feeling quite down followed as I began to question my future, wondering what I was going to do in order to lead a successful life and what hobbies I could take up instead of my beloved running and football. After some soul searching and serious grown-up thinking, where I fully considered the surgeon's professional opinion, however, one stubborn thought came through loud and clear: I would indeed run another marathon and if I could only ever do one more, it had to be the London Marathon. I had to at least try and this would show the world that I was back, that I wasn't beaten.

It was already too late for that year's London Marathon and besides I was nowhere near ready anyway so I started to form a plan for the following year. I considered entering the ballot, realising that the chances were that I would not get in, such is the demand for places, but that this might be my only ever chance to do what I had said I would do so many years ago. I decided to honour an old promise made by my younger self, sitting in front of the telly, surrounded by *Star Wars* toys and comics (probably). I decided that it had to be a charity run – but which charity? I think you already know the answer to that.

And it had to be a good one, a plan so brilliant that the British Heart Foundation couldn't possibly ignore me. You see I had previously applied twice to run the London Marathon for them over the years and both times was turned down. On the application form I had rather half-heartedly explained why they should allow me onto their team by telling them about Grandma and how I would stage quizzes, cake sales and the like. All the general stuff and, looking back, this was a mistake as I was not being inventive or imaginative enough. I learnt later that the BHF have thousands of people applying for only 300 spots or so. Much like sending your CV in for a job you really want, your application has to stand out and really grab their attention. Cake sales and quizzes are all well and good and, indeed, they are actually great ways to raise money but, application form wise, they have heard it all before. I had to come up with something different to make my application form stand out from the rest, catch their attention and then persuade them to give me a spot on the team. It was clear that I had to think outside the box to really get their attention and I started to brainstorm. An early thought designed to totally defy my surgeon was to run the London Marathon with a football but then realised that it was one of the worst ideas I have ever had – ask anyone I have ever played football with and they will tell you that my close control is non-existent at the best of times. To take a football onto a course with about 40,000 other runners would lead to carnage. An awful idea indeed and I put that one in the metaphorical bin pretty quickly.

I considered running the length of Great Britain with the London Marathon in the middle on my way south but discounted that on costs and annual leave grounds. At over 900 miles it would have taken too long and cost me too much money on places to stay and food to eat. Yes I could have cycled it a lot quicker but I wanted to run, it had to be a run. I actually still quite fancy that idea but I will probably cycle the length of Britain as part of a future project, just as something different to do.

I then considered running around the Isle of Wight or the length of Hadrian's Wall, but again had to discount them as a thought crossed my mind: Grandma was a London girl and so really the whole thing should be London focused and London based. These two ideas are also stored away for future projects.

And then the idea finally hit. An idea so brilliant, exciting and challenging that surely they would notice me and put me in their team. I was sitting at my parents' house and watching a preview for the 2012 London Olympics and Para-Olympics on the tellybox when the River Thames was shown. It struck a chord with me instantly. What was more of a London landmark than the River Thames?

One of the few bonuses of being stuck on your backside and unable to get about very easily is that the people around you collect things like your laptop, food and drink and bring it to you to make life easier. And so it was that I took a slurp of orange squash, because I could, replaced the cup on the floor and headed for a well-known search engine. Upon quick research, I learnt that the River Thames is 184 miles long and runs between a field in Gloucestershire and the Thames Barrier. There was even an official National Trail path alongside it. How about I ran the whole length of the Thames and then join the BHF team for the Virgin London Marathon? All I'd have to do is follow the signs. It would be easy.

On the surface of it, this was an idea that had a lot going for it so, when I was back on my feet, feeling 45 stone heavier and glaringly unfit, I filled in the official application form, bought a stamp and ran it down to the post box. By which I mean I climbed enthusiastically from the chair at my living room table, grabbed my door keys, ran down the stairs and practically fell into a sweaty pathetic heap, gasping and breathless, by the post box which can only be about 100 metres away. An awful but true story and one which illustrated perfectly just how daft my idea was fitness-wise. I was so unfit and heavy that looking back I am surprised that my doctor said it should be OK to even give this a go. Anyway, I had spent a lot more time on the application form this time around and had invested more time and effort in explaining how I'd raise them their money, explained about the personal motivation (Grandma) and came up with a few other fundraising ideas, including leg waxing, quizzes and cake sales. I really worked hard on it. Yes, I included some of the same ideas as before but I pitched it to them differently. That's a big lesson for anyone who is planning something similar – take the time to get the pitch right. The BHF requested that I raise £2000 and so I pledged to raise them £3000. My cunning plan worked and I was rather unsurprised in August 2012 to receive a letter telling me I had made the team.

I was still on a massive high from the fabulous 2012 London Olympic and Para-Olympic Games. I had been utterly caught up in it all and was so inspired by what I saw across a multitude of sports. I had been worried that we would mess it up when it was announced that London was to be the host city, I think a lot of people were, but actually we didn't and it was tremendous. As the closing ceremony concluded and, in the privacy of my bachelor pad, I resolved to make this run "my Olympic Games". I was highly excited, right up until practical things like reality caught up with me.

It is all very well making it onto the team but I still didn't have much of a clue whether or not I was actually able to run, what with everything my body had been through in recent times and my confidence shaken by the fact that my wobbly body had struggled to make it to the post box that night. I started training to see how it all went and was pleased that my body, despite the inevitable lack of fitness, held up and seemed willing to give this a go. It was a grand night when I first jogged for no more than a minute on the treadmill at a local gym. It was such a slow pace that I was practically walking but I was so happy and had a big old smile right across my face, which hopefully took away from the fact that I was breathing and sweating really heavily within about 10 seconds. Naturally I found the training tough but I was pleased that surgery-wise my body was holding up OK and that it was just a case of losing weight and putting the work in. I have run for so many years and incurred so many injuries that I know my fitness will return after a while and was content to rely on that experience gained. Sure, it was incredibly frustrating that my body was currently unable to do what it had done before and it was difficult to be patient, but patient I was and I worked out a plan to build up my training to eventually what I would need to be doing if I ever stood any chance at all of being successful. I progressed to running a short distance very slowly indeed, even by my standards as I knew it would be a challenge but I knew that I needed to test the toe to see if it could take the impact. After all, these surgeons are reputed to know their job pretty well and he had made it clear that he didn't think I would be able to run long distances again. As a result I was quite nervous the first few times I headed out and ran the streets but it turned out that my foot could take the pounding and stress of running, for now at least, so I cautiously stepped it up and, fairly soon, I was able to run for half an hour with no real trouble, albeit very slowly.

It had been quite some time since I last ran for miles on end and I enjoyed the freedom of not being cooped up in my flat. It felt liberating to be back doing what I term as "my thing" again, delighted that I could at least run this far after the toe fusion surgery. I generally ran alone which I found really beneficial. I work in a busy office, you see, and all day phones ring, people want to talk to you, emails are coming in. I learnt once again to love the idea of solitude and a little bit of peace and quiet. One thing I did do however was carry my mobile phone and this is something that I always urge people to do – getting hit by that car taught me that things can happen quickly, with no warning. Literally the whole world can change in a second. I think it is vital for all runners, old and young, fast and slow, male and female, to carry some ID and their phone because you just never know what you will encounter out there. And it doesn't have to be you either – you might come across someone who has collapsed and need to telephone for an ambulance or perhaps someone might be acting suspiciously. Equally, of course, the local Accident and Emergency department might need to know who you are and call someone to inform them you have been injured and are in hospital. I put my phone on silent when out running so that I can have the best of both worlds; I am unlikely to realise my phone is ringing or that you have sent me a text message but equally I can call someone if I need to. It also means in this day and age of camera phones that if something catches your eye you can take a photo, by which I do not mean attractive people and I am not encouraging you to take photos of people you fancy in the street. You can cast those people one of your winning smiles and ask for their number – you know, the old-fashioned way of letting someone you like know you like them. My personal tip for impressing the ladies is to catch their eye, panic, stammer and look the other way as you run off. As a result my love life has been remarkably consistent over the years. You can have that tip for free, a gift from me to you.

Anyway, I had company one night when a badger ran out from the bushes and alongside me for a short while. That was a new running experience for me and something to write about, which is what I have just done, obviously. That was a pleasant and a first-time experience for me. Sadly, there are always some people that have to be horrible and two or three times over the course of a fortnight, I experienced the same two lads hanging out of a car window as they drove past me in their mate's car shouting "Fatty! Oi, fatty!" amongst other things relating to my rather large frame. They even seemed to be claiming that I didn't have a father *and* was highly obese, with a particular fondness for eating pies, or words to that effect. How rude. It is difficult to know how to react when someone does that. Why would they need to? It was not a particularly nice experience and actually I admit to being a little upset by it. What is the point of it after all? It is unlikely that they were worried about my health and out of the kindness of their heart were trying to encourage me to lose some weight, I took the view that they were being rather less kind than that. But what to do? Parents always say to ignore the bullies at school and clearly these are not the sort of people that I would be thrilled about my sister marrying because they are mean. But I didn't want to ignore them, I wanted to give them something back. I build my life on a "be nice" policy so swearing at them wasn't really appropriate and besides they were now back in their car, presumably having a right laugh at my expense, so I settled on a sarcastic thumbs-up and smile, thinking to myself: "Nice one, lads. You have a go at someone whilst driving by at 40 miles per hour, giving me no chance of a decent comeback" and my reaction in their rear view mirror would have shown them the error of their ways, at least that's the hope.

Or perhaps the fact that I smiled at such an experience made me look a bit simple. Either way, I used this as a motivational tool for the rest of the run and, indeed, for quite a long time afterwards.

Not everyone was verbally abusive however. In fact most people who had heard what I was training for were incredibly enthusiastic and kind. Sure, I did get a few "you are crazy" comments but that was to be expected. When I told a friend of mine, Andy, he remarked that I truly was brilliantly bonkers, which I thought a great expression so I kept it in mind in case I ever wrote the book of my adventures. It would be a good film too, I think. Which raises an important question – who would play me? I am not sure who I would want to; could I play myself? Mind you, seeing as I have in my life been told that I look like both Sloth from *The Goonies* and Shrek, it might not be such a good idea. Maybe I will settle for a guest walk-on part in the background. It is probably for the best, all things being equal.

I guess when the film is commissioned by a major film production company, they would have ideas for who would be suitable for a film based on my life. I presume that it would have to be an actor who is a bit plump, talks a bit too fast and is bald. All that can be acted out of course but I am struggling to think of someone off the top of my head that I would be pleased about. I shall have to give this a bit of thought and get back to you.

I built the running up and up and after a few weeks of hard graft I was able to run an hour around my local park. I was brimming with optimism now, right up until I really started to think about the route and how far it was. The fact that I was telling everyone about it (in my defence, I had to, it was a charity fundraiser), meant that it was always on my mind so I even dreamt about it fairly often. In my dream I would just be running, running... running. Nothing else would happen really. It was the sort of dream you wake up from in the middle of the night and be grateful that it was only a dream and that the real event would be so much more exciting than that surely, then return to your slumber and dream the exact same dream again.

WHAT DO I NEED NEXT? DEFINITELY A SLOGAN!

Things had got real. Not only had I signed up to run a bloody long way but I also had to raise at least £3000 for an excellent charity and I was determined to do so. It made sense to start early and I started to plan events and appeals to get the word out there. I also wanted to make sure the project had a catchy title so that it would stick in people's minds.

Many years ago I was in a curry house in Leatherhead where I was drunkenly telling the people I was with about a project I was working on and how great it was. In the midst of my excited chattering I remarked to the girl I was trying to impress that it was a "great adventure" but then, without accepting or considering what I was about to say, I carried on "or do I mean edventure?" in what I like to think was a very Roger-Moore-as-James-Bond-kind-of-way. I am convinced that I raised one eyebrow as I said it but then seeing as I am not actually able to do that perhaps it is a false memory. Anyway she laughed, I laughed because she laughed and was rather attractive and like I say I was trying to impress her, and then everyone laughed when it was relayed to the table and they could see what I was up to. It was close to midnight by this time and we had all consumed a lot of alcohol. The girl and I didn't work out but I had come up with a great word. It wasn't the first time this sort of thing had happened. A flatmate and I once got drunk and came up with a plan to get me voted Prime Minister at the next election. Included in this were terms such as "think ahead, vote for Ed!" and "he sure is handsome, vote Ed Vanson!". To be fair at the time they sounded like brilliant slogans and I suspect that is the beauty of alcohol. So many times in life I have looked back and thought that the booze has a lot to answer for and not always in a bad way. I will still use those slogans if I ever run for Prime Minister by the way. Anyway, the term "edventure" had been rattling away in the back of my mind ever since and this seemed like the best time to give it a use and to coin it officially. And so "edventure running" was born.

I wonder if I can get the word "edventure" into the English dictionary.

Two thousand and thirteen years anno domini is a time of vast social networking and I utilised them as often as I could to approach people and ask them to follow my project and to tell everyone how I was getting on, not to mention sharing ideas. I set up an email address (edventurerunning@hotmail.co.uk) and a Facebook page called Edventure Running and spread the word. I had a fairly dormant twitter account (@edvanson6) which I reactivated, again with the intention of putting the word out there. I tweeted often about my plans and asked people to retweet. After much patience and many hours spent in front of my computer I was starting to get tweets and friend requests from people I didn't know. It was working but to be honest I had found this a real challenge. Obviously I am not famous or well known and therefore I don't have a following or people hanging onto my words. If someone famous decided to do this run then he or she would probably have a publicity machine behind him or her, and fair dues too, but this was just me, organising things from my living room table in my flat and sitting around in my pants. That is not to sound negative, incidentally, it is merely to say that I had to spend many hours myself approaching people, being knocked back or ignored by most, to tell people what I was up to and to ask them to support me in some way. It was often exhausting and even demoralising when people just didn't bother to reply or did so to say that they were not interested in my project. I realised after a few non responses that this was all part of the challenge. Not everyone was going to be interested, some people would hear what I was up to and think "so what?" I understood that once I thought it through. At first I had naively thought that everyone would just get on board and be really impressed by what I was trying to do, but life doesn't work like that. I resolved to concentrate on the good news, not the bad stuff and just keep going. This was not going to work out if I dwelt on the negatives. It felt a bit like when I was briefly persuaded to get involved in internet dating and got hardly any replies when I approached the ladies. There is no point in letting it get you down, you get on with it all. Although I am not true to my words, because after a while of not receiving any replies on a well-known dating website I just threw a sulk and closed my account down so it is a case of "do as I say not as I do" on that one. Really it is important to stay focused.

And I really did stay focused. I wanted to get cracking early on with raising the sponsorship money and, hey no time like the present, so I organised the first fundraising event with the help of Aldabella beauty salon in Epsom, which I contacted. I figured I needed to make a statement of intent, a mission statement if you will. It seemed to make sense to show how serious I was about all this, that I was prepared to suffer for the sake of my project but also something that would get people to notice me. And so it was that on Saturday 15th December 2012 I had my legs waxed.

The whole point of waxing is to remove the hair from its root and is accomplished by spreading a wax thinly over the skin. A cloth or paper strip is applied and pressed firmly to the wax. Then the waxee is basically physically assaulted by the waxer with the strip being ripped quickly against the direction of the hair growth. This removes the wax and the hair.

And if that sounds painful, that's because it is. It bloody hurts. It is even worse when you have an audience, believe me. Enjoying the spectacle were the photographer for the *Sutton and Epsom Guardian*, a few interested observers and the chap who updates the What's on in Epsom Twitter handle. So my painful afternoon made it into the local news, although I asked them to mention my entire project too.

I'll never forget the moment Beauty Therapist Laura took the first strip off my left shin, it wasn't the funniest moment of my life thus far and I admit to yelping a little. I won't be waxing my legs anytime soon and I salute people that wax regularly, that's for sure. When the manager of Aldabella, Lucy, asked how I was feeling mid-wax, I responded with "like I am being assaulted" which actually she found amusing. It was horrible, especially on my hamstrings. I am happy to say that my legs have remained hairy ever since that experience and shall be remaining that way thank you very much. An interesting side story to this and something that you might want to bear in mind for any sponsorship you may do in the future is that as soon as I mentioned that I would be waxing my legs for charity, I was contacted by a few people suggesting I don't do that but actually really push the boundaries by having what is known in the trade as a boyzillian. Or as we all know it, the famous "Back, sack and crack wax", which involves the removal of all hair from the lower back, penis, scrotum, buttocks and pubic areas. Yes, you are right, this does sound horrendous and I had absolutely no interest in this at all but I received quite a few comments from people telling me that they would sponsor me again if I agreed to do it.

Now, you will know that I was dedicated to this project and had to raise at least £3000 but this created quite a dilemma for yours truly to be honest – how far was I prepared to go to raise money for even such a brilliant charity as The British Heart Foundation? Like I say, I had no interest whatsoever in doing this, but if it was going to raise big money then perhaps I should put aside my feelings and just get on with it? In actual fact, was getting all the hair pulled out of intimate parts of my body the moral thing to do in this situation? I was in a real quandary so I decided to test the water a little and replied to one friend who asked, "how much would I have to raise to make this happen?" with the answer "get me £1000 pledged and we'll talk". He runs a pub in London so it wasn't necessarily the most unlikely of amounts. I never heard from him again about that and, to be honest, I was not totally upset about that either.

Put it this way, ever since a girl visibly winced and uttered an involuntary "ugh" with a real look of horror when I took my shirt off on Ryde beach on the Isle of Wight one hot summer's day quite a few years ago, I feel uncomfortable about going topless in public. With that experience often on my mind, getting the boys out of the barracks in front of a total stranger so that she can remove all the hair from them is unlikely to make me feel too good. I live to fight another day on that one. Thank God my friend didn't call my bluff though, I hate to think what would have happened. One last point – how would I have proved I had had it done? I would not have allowed cameras or a camcorder etc. in the room with me in that situation and there is no way in the world that I would have dropped my trousers and proved that one night in my friend's pub either.

I bet when you picked this book up you didn't expect me to start talking about hairless scrotums and dropping my trousers in pubs and the like.

Incidentally that day on the Isle of Wight was one of the most horrendous moments of my life, my thinking being "well, I am not trying to impress her but is that really how girls see me?" Were there other women on the beach equally horrified by the sight of my naked torso? Crikey. My friends were not much help either, they thought it was bloody hilarious.

I knew that I had to press on, now that I had people's attention, so I organised a Christmas Quiz at the Coopers Arms in Fulham. There is an old saying of "if you don't ask, you don't get" and I certainly embraced that. I wrote letters asking for donations of raffle and team prizes to lots of different companies and many responded. Sure I didn't hear back from quite a lot but percentage-wise I had a satisfactory response rate.

I ended up with several teams and the quiz was led by the pub landlord, another chap called Ed, who took great delight in describing me as fat when he was on the microphone. I admit that it stung in front of so many people but I let it go. If I am so fat it will be even tougher to run as far as I planned, making it more unlikely that I will succeed and so people may be more inclined to sponsor me or sponsor me more, so I merely used that comment as fuel and as motivation when the going got tough in the weeks and months ahead. When it is a horrible day outside, one has to find something within his or herself as motivation to get out the door and train and that memory was certainly something I used on occasion. I guess that I should thank that particular landlord for the motivation. Thanks Ed!

Anyway the quiz and raffle went well, making about £400 for the night's work. I then repeated the trick at work on a smaller scale and raised about £200 with the added attraction of a cake sale, where I persuaded people to bake cakes and donate them, with a suggested donation of 50 pence per item. I designed, wrote and led this quiz myself and threw in a very cunning trick question, which was "In what year was Queen Elizabeth the Second crowned at St Paul's Cathedral?" the answer of course, is that she wasn't. Her coronation took place at Westminster Abbey in 1953. I am not sure that anyone got that answer right and they all groaned and called me silly names in a friendly fashion when I read the answer out later on.

My biggest problem was reading the question out without giving away the fact it was a trick but I am proud that I pulled it off. It was a nice, new experience for me when I led the quiz that day. At the start of the quiz, I explained how it was all going to pan out and also that it was all a part of a bigger project. Some people clapped and cheered me when I said that I hoped to run the length of the River Thames and then run a marathon but I laughed that off and just replied with a jokey "no need to clap me, I haven't done it yet!" people laughed and wished me luck when they got the chance over the course of the afternoon. A light-hearted problem I also had was with the team names – naturally every team had one they designed themselves. A team of my colleagues, who had already told me they planned to stitch me up in front of everyone, named themselves "four chaps on a fact hunt". I will let you say that out loud a few times but I recommend you don't if your mother is nearby. You can imagine how hard I had to concentrate when I said that one out loud over the course of the afternoon. I was told afterwards that some people were cheating by looking up the answers on their mobile phones or by looking over another team's shoulders. Assuming that is true, that really would annoy me. I saw no evidence of cheating at all but it is something for you to bear in mind if you ever put on a quiz. I wonder how that could be enforced though – I'd be highly reluctant to tell everyone to turn their phone off before asking the first question, as the competitors could be expecting an important call or something could happen. I don't know if I really have an answer for that one but cheating would be easy in this day and age and there must be a way of combating it somehow.

At all times and on all promotional posters, I told people what I was intending to do and for whom. I basically bored people with it until they sponsored me. And it worked; sponsorship came in from all over the place and I was starting to realise how much I had actually taken on, although I was making decent progress. This was a big challenge, no doubt about it.

And I had to do all this whilst training. The 2012/2013 winter was a cold one, especially if you were out running in it. My training was pretty much every day and for a while my body really suffered with the mileage and repeated effort. The whole project took over my life as I started to really feel the pressure to get fit enough and then raise the money I needed to. However I was so determined to do this. Sometimes the run became boring so I would try and switch things up a bit so that I stayed interested and was not doing the same thing over and over, it might be as simple as a long run in the gym on a treadmill or running the usual route but the other way. All this probably explains why, early on Christmas Day 2012, I dressed up as Santa Claus and went for a short local run. This was to be one of my favourite runs ever. As I ran I was beeped by passing cars, had "Merry Christmas" shouted at me and I high-fived several people. It was a very pleasant experience to meet two young girls who were walking with their dad who were so excited to see me that they ran up to me shouting, "Santa! Hello Santa! Santa!" I stopped of course and high-fived the first one who presumably had a great story to tell her friends when she returned to school. The other little girl sadly became a little overwhelmed by the fact she was meeting Santa Claus and promptly burst into tears as she got closer, hugging her dad ever tighter and refusing my high-five. I felt really bad about that but hope when she looked back on it she enjoyed her moment meeting one of the most famous people in the world. Santa, I mean, not me.

I had taken the opportunity to have my photo taken just before leaving for this run and had updated the edventure Facebook page to say that I was heading out for a run and asking people to say hello if they saw me. My sister Lucy shared this link on her personal Facebook page and a friend of hers replied to say that he had seen me but no-one in his house had believed he had just seen Santa running past the window! It was such a great experience, this run, and I would love to do it again, even if the fake beard did get more than slightly itchy when mixed with sweat. It really did clear my mind and re-invigorated me mentally.

As anyone who has ever trained for anything will know, some days it can be tough to get the motivation to get out and go for a run, especially when the alarm goes off very early in the morning, you are warm in bed and you can hear the rain belting against the bedroom window. And then when you finally do get up and leave for a run, you may find it is snowing as well. It can be tough but I always try and remind myself that this is the sort of day that earns you finisher medals. So much work has to be put in, in order to get that moment, that beautiful moment, when you cross the finish line and realise your dream. But I had the motivation here, on days like these. I believed in it all so much that I never really struggled to get out and do the training. Some days I didn't want to, sure, of course there were days like that, but at the same time I still cannot remember a single day when I rolled over, turned the alarm off and went back to sleep because I couldn't be bothered to run or because it was too cold. You get out what you put in and all that. And, in addition to a superb and funny run that Christmas morning, which really refreshed me mentally, I always had the powerful memory of being called fat, which tended to pump me up and get me out of the door as well.

TEDSTOCK 2013

I love live music and have been going to gigs for years. In early 2013, I realised that I knew a few people in bands and it created an idea. It was too good an opportunity – to put my own fundraising gig on was a highly exciting thought and so I organised tedstock at The Grey Horse in Kingston Upon Thames and arranged for Heartstring to support the Borderline Artistic. I organised this part of the night well. These are two cracking bands and if you get a chance to see them live, I urge you to do exactly that. As I stood there watching the band, neatly attired in my red British Heart Foundation hoodie, I thought to myself "I made this happen". And I had. I had done well to get two bands and even a smattering of people to watch them. This was my doing and I could be pleased with that. I had never put on a gig before so I had taken a step into the unknown and pulled it off, to a certain extent anyway. The evening raised about £150 so it wasn't a failure in the slightest but I could have done so much better.

When I thought back to what I had done and subsequently why so few people had turned up, I realised that where I failed was on the promoting side. Only about ten people turned up, although many more had promised to do so. My biggest mistake was taking their word at face value and becoming complacent. I didn't do enough work in putting it out there. It all left a bit of a sour taste in my mouth because I realised where I had gone wrong too late. Still, lessons have been learnt, experience gained and I'll stage tedstock again someday, having gained some valuable knowledge on what I should have done and how I should have done it. It will be better promoted next time, I assure you of that, but it was further progress, more money raised and I was really starting to gather some momentum now.

TRYING TO FIND A ROUTE

You would be safe to assume that geographically the route from Source to the Thames Barrier would be pretty easy to organise but the route along the famous river was proving to be surprisingly problematic. All kinds of different daily mileage and ideas were designed and discarded. Eventually after many hours of researching, procrastinating and indecisiveness I settled on the following plan: Source – Lechlade – Newbridge – Oxford – Wallingford – Tilehurst – Henley on Thames – Windsor – Kingston Upon Thames – Putney – Tower Bridge and then finishing naturally at the Thames Barrier.

I also had to be fair to the people that care about me too. The biggest example of this is my parents, who actually seem to quite like me. They expressed real concern at my plans and the amount of stress it would place on my body. Equally, of course, they were very supportive of my plans to fundraise for the British Heart Foundation.

I told them that I would put the plan together and let them know it first, a deal I stuck to. I went back to the drawing board and got to work on the questions they had asked, which were actually very relevant, some of which I had overlooked entirely. The lesson I learnt here is not to assume that I have thought of everything and have all the answers. A different perspective and mindset will look at things from an alternative angle and this is very beneficial in ensuring that you are fully prepared ahead of the off. I was lucky that my brother Richard is a manager in the Health and Fitness industry and is more than adequately qualified to advise me on training, recovery and nutrition. That sort of contact was, and always will be, essential to any project of this kind. To achieve something like this requires a lot of help and I was very lucky to have that in abundance.

I became aware that I would also need a lot of help when I was actually on the Thames. How would I move my kit bag along between pit stops for example? That was quickly sorted by the brilliant Rachel Davis, the volunteer fundraising manager for Oxfordshire and Gloucestershire, who I found on Twitter. Rachel really bought into the project and arranged some of her volunteers to move my bag to my next stop while I was out west. Some friends and my parents said they would be able to help with that as I got closer to London. These were essential developments and made my life a lot easier as a result. One kind lady who wishes to remain anonymous said that she would not sponsor me but that she recognised that I would be spending a heck of a lot of my own money on running costs (excuse the pun, although to be fair I wish I had thought of that one earlier). She donated £50 and this was indeed put towards equipment and the like. That was a lovely gesture and was something I hadn't even thought about, let alone something I didn't expect. It all seemed to be going my way so far.

Naturally I had to find a place to stay each night. I spent a lot of time surfing the internet looking for places and asking for a discount. Most would not discount my room but would offer a free breakfast for example. Curiously, when I contacted the New Inn near Lechlade they promised me that they would do "what they could" and let me know when I arrived. I made a mental note to expect maybe a free couple of meals at best, which I'd be very pleased with. All costs came out of my pocket, you see, not what I fundraised, so if I could save anything at all, I'd be delighted. They had been really helpful and friendly on the phone and so on a whim and added to the fact that they were based very close to where I'd be running, at a highly convenient stopping point, I agreed to stay there. I had a good feeling with them.

With my kit bag travel organisation being now organised, I approached various companies to help me with what I needed. My local chemist provided me with a first aid kit, cold spray, deep heat and an array of things to help me stay healthy and to avoid being bunged up so to speak or, if I was, to not be too un-bunged up, so to speak.

A brilliant running store in Ashtead, Surrey, called Run to Live (www.runtolive.co.uk) were superb and invited me in for a chat, where they bestowed upon me their considerable knowledge. I left the shop armed with a lot more knowledge, not to mention bags of extra equipment which were either donated or heavily discounted, on the proviso that I mention them on the edventure running Facebook page and wherever else I could. I was and am more than happy to do so. I still shop there now and it is truly a brilliant place for any runner to use.

CELEBRITY EDVENTURE
SUPPORTERS

I couldn't be too serious for too long, I get bored and distracted very easily and so it was that, after deciding that I wanted some celebrity support, I wrote to such people as Her Majesty Queen Elizabeth the Second, Prime Minister David Cameron and Mayor of London Boris Johnson and told them my plans. I received a reply from all of them and will never forget how exciting it was to check my letterbox one day to find a letter with a Buckingham Palace stamp on the back and subsequently a letter from the Queen's first lady wishing me luck on behalf of Her Majesty. Mayor Johnson wrote me a personal letter which was really gratefully received. I thought about writing back to him and asking if I could stop for a photo with him as I would be running past his office, if I got that far, but never did get round to it which to this day I deeply regret. The most disappointing one was from David Cameron's secretary who wished me luck and wrote a perfectly decent, friendly letter, one which I cannot have any complaints about at all but which also said basically that Mr Cameron had not seen my letter, nor would he, as he was too busy. Now, I am not a smart man but nor am I stupid. I am well aware that the people that wrote back to me were probably just signing a letter written by their secretaries and knew nothing at all about my run and project. But that is OK because there is always the chance that they did indeed read my letter. I would never have known whether or not Mr Cameron had, so they may as well have just lied and said "Mr Cameron is a bit busy running the country at the moment but was really impressed by your letter and project and instructed me to write and wish you good luck". Let's be honest, he almost certainly would have if I had been famous. So, that was a bit of a disappointment, but there you go. It was still a letter that I was very grateful to receive from Number Ten and obviously I kept it as a souvenir of what I was trying to achieve. I also wrote to the Chief Executive of Surrey County

Council who had recently been championing charity work and he not only replied wishing me well but also sponsored me personally, although I was surprised when he signed off his comment on my donation page with a kiss. However the biggest and most incredibly exciting surprise was a six-second video, organised by my friend Andy, from Olympic hero Mo Farah who actually addressed me by name and told me to "go get 'em". This was such a brilliant thrill and I played the video back again and again, delighted at the fact that, for the briefest of moments, Mo Farah, the *actual* Mo Farah, had known who I was.

My final material problem was that of kit. I knew that I had to wear comfortable running kit but I wanted to stand out so that people would ask what I was up to and hopefully sponsor me. It was obvious that the British Heart Foundation had an official colour of red so there was my answer: I would wear all red. Being keen to help a small company seemed a good idea as they might be more willing to charge me less than their larger counterparts and besides I like the idea of helping the smaller companies. So, after a lot of internet research, I contacted a company called Hungdrawn Vinyl who are based in Ewell, Surrey. The manager there, a fellow called Simon Brocklehurst, was very helpful and agreed to meet me for a chat. Together we selected my kit and he arranged for the design created by my sister-in-law Emma to be transferred to the shirts, at a reduced rate, in return for the Hungdrawn name to be included on the shirt as sponsorship.

The last fortnight before I left for the start of the Thames was taken up with last minute training, desperate emails to people that had said they might sponsor me and checking and rechecking my plans. Oh and going on local radio. I had contacted my local radio station to tell them what I was up to and asking if they would support me in some way or another. As a result one beautiful Wednesday morning in April 2013 my pre-recorded interview was played on the Radio Jackie breakfast show, exposing my dulcet tones to the whole of South East London. Donations really started to come in as what I brilliantly entitled "edstart" got closer, as they tend to in these situations. It is almost a case of people wanting to see if you are serious or not. Slowly I edged closer and closer until, on April 3rd 2013, I finally reached my target of £3000. It goes without saying that I was absolutely delighted with this and was relieved that I had raised what I had promised. That said, I seemed to have a lot of momentum at the moment so I raised my target amount regularly as more and more sponsorship came in. A lot of the pressure was now off me and I hadn't even started the run yet so I was able to just train.

Run, run, run, every day was the same. At the peak of my training I was trying to run hard twice a day, once in the morning before work and once in the evening after work. That didn't last long as my body really struggled and on several occasions I genuinely thought that I was getting a stress fracture on my left foot and shin splints in both legs. Worried, I went back to training once a day and also stepped up the swimming to keep my fitness up. I was very worried that I wouldn't be able to complete this run, I'll be honest with you, and the thought of failing filled me with absolute dread. And then my friend Craig told me that he had been diagnosed with cancer and was adopting the motto "no matter the odds, never give up". Naturally I wanted to support him and so asked if I could also use his motto for the run. Craig said he was fine with this and so I had it adopted for edventure running as my official motto and then had it tattooed on my left arm by a chap named Darrell Hobbs, who works out of Shutes Tattoo Studio in Carshalton, Surrey (if you are interested look up Darrell Hobbs Tattoo on Facebook, his work is brilliant). This would prove to be a useful motivational tool for me – I was confident that, when things got as tough on the Thames as I expected them to, I only had to look at my arm to re-gain a sense of perspective and motivation. It was only running after all.

EDSTART

April 7th came round very quickly indeed and soon enough it was time to travel to the edstart at the source. I had by this time fully discussed the project with my parents and answered their questions and concerns well enough to put their minds at rest. They agreed to drive me west as their sponsorship donation.

I stayed at theirs the night before, the same house that I had grown up in, and was treated to a meal high in carbohydrates and plenty of encouragement. I was very excited and pleased to be able to talk about the project openly at last – because I didn't have all the answers, I hadn't really discussed it with them too much before. I knew they were worried and I didn't want to give them any further cause for concern by giving a vague answer. Now I had all the answers, I was delighted to try and give them a full picture of my intended project.

It made sense to give a detailed itinerary to the friends I would be staying with en-route and to my parents. This way people would know where I was meant to be and when along the Thames. Once they had it, I uploaded a brief copy of the plan onto the edventure Facebook page and subsequently received a lot of support from an ever increasing number of my friends and supporters.

Before leaving the next morning I recorded a very short video message to the same Facebook page, thanking everyone for their support and promising I would do my best to not let them all down. I was nervous and excited, wanting to be off.

Plenty of banter in the car on the way to the Cotswolds soon settled nerves and if anything greatly contributed to my excitement levels. We arrived in Ewen at the Wild Duck Inn during the early afternoon and, seeing as I was excited and that it was a nice day, decided to head to the source of the Thames to start there and then. The thing with that end of the Thames trail is that it is pretty remote.

The source was about two miles away and I'd have to come back past the Wild Duck Inn to carry on the trail. It made sense to do that very short part of the run first, to make day two a little easier logistically. So that's exactly what I did, the first big decision of the actual run was a smart one.

We parked at the 'Thames Head' public house, which some people believe is the actual source of the Thames. Officially however the source is to be found roughly a mile away under an Ash tree in a meadow, marked by the Thames Conservators. There is also a sign showing that the Thames Barrier is 184 miles away, which brought it home a little. It is totally impossible by the way to stand at the source in a totally dry meadow and not think of the Thames in places such as Windsor or as it flows past the Houses of Parliament for example. It is an obvious thing to say but it is an amazing contrast.

Mum, Dad, Sis and I all made sure that the moment was captured on both film and video to share with supporters and sponsors before, suddenly, it was time. Fourteen months of planning and preparation had literally come down to this one moment. I took a last contemplative look at my surroundings and then took the first of many steps, the last of which would hopefully see me arrive at the Thames Barrier. As I ran off I contemplated staging a comedy fall or faking an injury, just because I am hilarious like that, but then I realised that actually by doing that I probably would do myself a mischief and that would be a terrible thing. Imagine after all this work I hurt myself by throwing myself to the ground pretending to be injured and not being able to get out of the first field, let alone complete the trail because I was actually injured? I decided to play it safe and just run. Life seemed safer that way.

RUN A MILE, STOP AT THE NEXT PUB

That first run didn't go very far. In fact I ran a mile and stopped at the pub, where I stretched and waited for the others to catch me up. When they finally got to the Thames Head, we had a quick drink each (an orange juice for me) and I studied a large Thames trail map of the area that is on the wall in there before being interrupted by, and seemingly laughed at by, the very rude bar lady. She made it clear that she didn't fancy my chances of completing my task, let's put it that way. Then again if I was going to run a mile and stop for a drink all the time it was going to take me months probably. This visit had had to be done though, and I had been determined to visit this pub as part of my run – all the research I had conducted is conclusive that the source of the Thames lies in that meadow as signposted but some people still believe that actually the Thames Head pub marks the, well, head of the Thames. I needed to cover all eventualities as, if I was going to do this, I was going to do it properly. So I did.

I was pretty confident, having briefly studied the map that I knew the way back to the Wild Duck Inn, my first night's stay, and it was only a short run anyway. Besides navigation has always been a strong point of mine. So I turned right out of the Thames Head car park and onto the A433 where the lack of a decent footpath to run on only became more of a concern when I realised that every car on the road was determined to travel at speeds far in excess of the speed limit. I ran uphill and down for what seemed like ages and started to worry that something was not quite right. Why could I not see the Hamlet of Ewen? And why did no signpost mention the Hamlet of Ewen for that matter? Suddenly a large aeroplane swopped down towards a field next to me. I was stunned and, thinking I was witnessing something truly dramatic, a hijack or a major international incident perhaps, I stopped in a convenient lay-by, peeking through the bushes to investigate and to check my route. What I saw astounded me – it was an airport. I later found out that it was the Cotswolds Airport. This should have rung alarm bells but didn't – stubbornly and arrogantly I still believed that I was on the right road and so on and on I went. It was only when I came to another signpost that mentioned I was running in the direction of Bath that I stopped, swore at myself and checked the guidebook properly, before running back the way I had come and taking the correct route, about 100 yards or so from the Thames Head pub. By the time I had got to the Wild Duck Inn, my parents and sister were out driving the lanes trying to find me. Great start, Vanson!

In total I ran about 10km extra that day. It served as a very useful lesson to not be complacent or arrogant. It was lucky that I had made this sort of mistake on the roads and not actually further out when I was all alone. If I was going to complete this project I had to respect it and do it properly. I learnt my lesson and, from there on in, every night, I thoroughly read up on the next day's route so I knew where I was going and what to expect.

Mum, Dad and Lucy had driven past me a couple of times and videoed me running and shouting encouragement at me. Such support was very welcome and, when I ran past the farms and cottages of Ewen and arrived at the very attractive Wild Duck Inn, I thanked them for it over dinner. I was also bought a pint of ale by a man who had seen my running shirt and was impressed with my project. Free pints of ale were not the target when I had the shirts made up but were a happy consequence anyway.

Later I watched as Mum, Dad and Lucy pulled out of the car park and headed for home. I was now on my own, no physical support team with me. It was me versus the length of the River Thames. Things had just got real.

EDSTART DAY 2: WHAT'S THE WORST THAT COULD HAPPEN?

I awoke the next day after a fine sleep and had a great breakfast of porridge. My bag was left in the bar ready to be transported and I walked the 400 yards odd back to the Thames Trail with a Canadian couple who were proud to be walking a part of the famous Thames. I soon put them in their place when I told them what I was up to! They were fairly astonished but supportive and wished me well. And soon I was off and running in the direction of Cricklade, 12 and a quarter miles away. I'll always remember the thrill of starting that day: 14 months I'd been waiting for this and, if I could pull it off, it'd be one heck of an achievement.

At that stage there were a few people around, walking their dogs or out for a stroll. Everyone said hello as I jogged past and I was struck by how friendly everyone was in the country.

Through the kissing gates, open meadows and over bridges, I plodded along. When planning this run I imagined that I'd spend every day and every step thinking about how far I'd still have to run to get to the Thames Barrier, but actually I was taking it one landmark at a time. I very rarely thought about completing the whole run, the next little victory was what I was aiming for.

The Thames at its most infant is an incredible sight. It looks so small and serene, quite incapable of powering watermills and the like as they used to in ye olden days. Again I couldn't help but compare the sight in front of me to the only Thames I had ever known in London. I crossed the Thames via a footbridge at the Cotswold Water Park towards Ashton Keynes, where I marvelled at the Cotswold stone all around me and then ran past one of the four curious looking headless preaching crosses in the area and made a mental note to find out what their story was.

Running solo has its challenges, not least the lack of company. I countered this on the approach to Cricklade by pondering an important question, something that has been bothering me for quite a while: If Hannibal Lecter and Darth Vader got into a battle of stare off, who would win? To my mind it would probably be Lecter because, despite his quite obvious character flaws (cannibalism for example), I don't think he can be described as weak minded. He's probably a very stubborn fellow so it's very possible he'd beat Vader. But then again if he got annoyed and tried to instigate fisticuffs, Lecter would be in trouble as I don't think they are on the same physical level. But I think ultimately Hannibal Lecter would win as he is strong mentally and would have Lord Vader in a right old state.

Glad at having cleared that up, I ran into Cricklade town centre with a spring in my step, having unravelled that mystery. Cricklade is the first "proper" built-up area on the Thames so it is quite a significant landmark and one I was looking forward to seeing. Despite appearing an attractive place, I ran through the town quickly. I was not here on a sightseeing holiday, I was here on a mission and I needed to get to Lechlade, my home for the night. That was still eleven miles away, so despite being over half way through the day's planned route, there was no stopping, no resting. I ploughed on and headed further towards my destination and, hopefully, another pint of ale, free or otherwise. It is a pretty rural run to say the least between Cricklade and Lechlade and I saw almost no-one. The Thames Path is however very well signposted so I never felt any concern at possibly getting lost. Beautiful countryside provided a stunning backdrop to my plodding and it was a really satisfying day.

All was going well as I approached Upper Inglesham. It had been a brilliant day and I was making good progress in a decent time. Not that I cared about time. Time was irrelevant to me, all that mattered was each day's goal. The path was again well marked by the National Trust, so I was content. Tired, but content. I was basking in the satisfaction of a job nearly well done and followed the correct path into a field, a field that I would remember for a long time. As I got halfway across, I became aware that three cows were paying me an awful lot of attention. They didn't seem threatening so I continued towards the gate that had now come into view a short distance away. These cows were now clearly quite humpy however and a lot of mooing ensued as they moved slowly ever closer, one now blocking the path to the gate, the others approaching from different directions, a bit like a three-way cow pincer movement. I slowed right down and tried to play it cool, all the time looking to my left for an escape route if they attacked, which I still thought highly unlikely.

It doesn't happen in real life does it? Except it does, and suddenly they ran very fast at me, all three of them, causing a very bizarre scenario where I was running towards a river uttering a phrase that rhymes with "mucking sell" with three cows legging it after me, and me climbing high up a tree, sitting on a branch directly above the river that I was trying to run, and on which I stayed for fifteen minutes or so while I waited for them to get bored and go away. Once I was up there I had a little time to think and assess the situation and, once I knew that I was safe, barring the branch snapping of course, which even then would mean that I ended up in the Thames not in a field full of angry cows, I allowed myself to laugh at the absurdity of it all. I had never been chased by cows before and probably hadn't climbed a tree so fast since I was a young boy. I only became slightly alarmed at this situation when I realised that actually cows have been known to hurt and kill people before. And who do I call for assistance? I doubt it would be 999 and I have no idea at all who this field belongs to. What do I do? Just wait up here until they get bored then? Is that really my best plan of action? I am not the stupidest man in the world, I must be able to think of something so I donned my metaphorical thinking cap and got to work. Alas, I couldn't think of a decent idea so my plan basically involved waiting a few more minutes and then running away when they were not looking. It was a similar plan I adopted when I started at high school and some sixth formers had taken a dislike to me. It occasionally worked then and it would probably work now.

The beauty of social media again meant that I could tell my friends and supporters what had happened. I put up a status on the edventure page saying that "I am now hiding up a tree after annoying three cows and may be here some time!"

It is lucky that I had not banked on people being really worried about me as the responses I received to this status update were much more of an amused nature. I mean, these are lovely people so of course they would have been worried about me if I had actually been in danger but generally people found it a funny status update.

Those pesky cows were still pretty close by but appeared to have lost interest in me so very slowly I inched my way down the tree and then, when they had turned their heads, sprinted as fast as I possibly could to the nearby gate and freedom, all the while giggling like a school boy during sex education lessons.

I carried on giggling to myself all the way along the trail until I approached the A361 which I had been forewarned as a potentially dangerous part of my run. As I approached the last farm before this junction I became aware of my scenery again. Suddenly I was concerned to see a whole flock of sheep staring at me from quite a distance. Convinced that it couldn't happen again, I continued until a load of them ran towards me! This time my animal friends didn't seem so aggressive. It was almost like a pack of dogs protecting their land. It just seemed territorial.

I stopped and evaluated the situation whilst pretending to stretch, trying to hold off any embarrassment and make it appear to any passers-by that I knew what I was doing. But there were no passers-by and I was still in a field, involved in a face-off with some sheep. This wasn't what I was expecting and for the first ever time I found myself pondering just how much of a physical threat sheep are or can be. I doubt anyone has ever pondered that question before. And then, all of a sudden, and as if by magic, a local gentleman and his wife walked along from the direction I had just come from and I tagged along after fiddling with my backpack a little and checking my shoelaces were tied up so as not to look too stupid and like an out of my depth townie.

They still ran towards me of course, clearly it was that sort of day, but there was no emergency tree climbing needed, which was fortunate because they were not any trees around, believe me, I had looked. Again I leapt upon the chance to tell my knights in shining armour what I was up to and they were impressed. By now I had my silver running jacket on as I had belatedly realised that cows probably didn't like the colour red and I was covered in it. Anyway the upshot was that I had to tell them about it first without them asking. Any shyness has to go right out of the window in these situations – I wanted them to know about it so they might sponsor me. Around this time I had a few "anonymous" people sponsoring me on my edventure JustGiving page so it might even have worked. After a chat about running and me posing for a photo (turns out he was the warden for that particular stretch of the trail), I was given tips on how to get to Lechlade alongside such a busy road and, for a while, they even followed me in their car, making sure I was going in the right direction, which I thoroughly appreciated.

All the local advice tells you not to walk or run along the A361 between Upper Inglesham and Inglesham and, upon reaching the road, I can understand why. There is a pavement for a while and a grass verge in some parts but there is a blind bend; you have to cross the road twice, with no pedestrian crossing and the speed limit is 60 miles per hour. Yep, best to listen to the people that know and take a taxi or bus instead.

However I am incredibly stubborn and so, as I was running along the A361 between Upper Inglesham and Inglesham, with cars whizzing past me at great speeds, I resolved to not tell my parents about this bit until I got home. Still, it was only a mile or so and I ran it fairly quickly. It went so well this bit that it was almost a bit of an anti-climax to be honest. There is no doubt that I got lucky to a certain extent at least – sensibly I had decided to always start the run as early as possible, however far I had to run, to make as much use as possible of the daylight. So it was broad daylight and traffic seemed light. It was easy to see what was happening around me, drivers could see me and it was simple and quick to cross the road.

And cross the road I certainly did, down a road which signposted Inglesham Church. I'm told that it is a very attractive place to see, but again I knew what I was here to do. Maybe one day I'll return but for now I had to make it to Lechlade.

I carried on following the path after passing through a kissing gate and then entered a meadow which led to the remains of the Thames-Severn canal. I was now in Lechlade Riverside Park and, brilliantly, I saw my first boats on the Thames. Up ahead I could see the spire of St Lawrence and the 18th-century town bridge, which I prefer to refer to as Ha'Penny bridge as the locals do because they used to charge a toll to cross it. I made a left turn over the bridge and found myself in Lechlade, the highest point of the Thames.

I found the New Inn and checked in shortly afterwards. Testimony to the organisational genius of Rachel Davis was the fact that my kit bag was in the bar and waiting for me. That was good news, great news even, but it got better as Nick the hotel manager indeed looked after me as he had promised, giving me the en-suite room number 37 for free as he was impressed with what I was trying to accomplish. The room even came complete with a TV, double bed and the promise of the essential ingredient for the dreaded ice bath.

Ice baths are horrible, no point in trying to say otherwise. They hurt, are uncomfortable and are the most dreaded thing for anyone knowing that one is on the horizon but are famous for aiding physical recovery from strenuous exercise. They are there to be endured but never, ever enjoyed. However I received a super tip from Nicky at 'Run to Live' in Ashtead, which I'd like to share with you now: Run a cool bath and get in it. Don't make it too deep and add the ice slowly from a receptacle next to the bath. This doesn't give the body the shock it would normally but still gets the job done. I was further fortunate that my dad called me while I was in said bath to chat about the day just gone and to make sure that I had got into Lechlade safely. It was a great diversion for me, which is also vital when you are doing something so uncomfortable. I am not sure if he knew, until now, that he rang me when I was in the bath that day. Probably for the best.

Once I had completed the ice bath and stretched, I washed and changed before watching television and later heading down to the bar and watching the United v City derby game where I ate and sank a couple of beers. It was quite surreal when the barman shouted across the bar "Ed Vanson, is there an Ed Vanson here?" I thought that finally my time had come. Perhaps I had been spotted somewhere and I was being asked for an interview for a local paper or maybe Sky television wanted me on the evening news. As it turns out it was my aunt who was calling to see if she could pay my bar tab for me as a show of support. I'm not surprised really, she is that sort of aunt.

The local ales I tried were very nice and I drank a few more of them than I should have in celebration of a very satisfactory day. Then suddenly I thought I was going to be sick so I legged it back to my room to be on the safe side.

I liked the look of Lechlade and the people there were so friendly to me. One chap even gave me £10 for the charity pot when he saw my T-shirt as I arrived which was brilliant. Another lady gave me a fiver the next morning at breakfast when she asked what my plans were for the day ahead. She was also Canadian, so as far as I am concerned this was now getting international attention and I was a major star in Canada. As I set off east that morning I vowed to return for a longer stay one day.

Lechlade is laid out in such a way that one cannot help but imagine days of old, thanks to the small marketplace and coaching inns. I like it when pubs call themselves "coaching inns" to try and create an olde worlde atmosphere. I am quite a simple chap and one of my great pleasures in life is to sit in an old pub with a pint and feel the history around me. Usually of course these 'old' pubs are just 'new' themed pubs with a historic façade. In Lechlade it feels genuine, especially with the spire of St Lawrence so prominent. As I've said, Lechlade, (correctly pronounced "Letchlade" – I know because I got it wrong and was given a lesson by a local) is the highest point of the Thames that barges could reach; back in the days Cotswold stone and Gloucestershire cheeses were loaded up to travel to London. So I guess, in a running sense, I'd done the hard work getting to this point and it should all be downhill from here on in. That wasn't necessarily a metaphor I was happy with but at the time it made sense when I considered it in the purely geographical running sense.

MEETING OLD FATHER THAMES

I bade Lechlade a fond farewell the next morning and headed towards my first photo stop of the day; St John's Lock. This was an important point for two reasons – firstly it was the first lock of my edventure and also because it houses the statue of Old Father Thames himself. It was a slightly surreal experience to be honest but I was pleased to pay my respects and have the obligatory photo taken with him by the lock keeper, who was so impressed by my challenge that he gathered a group of his friends to cheer me off again on my run, shouting encouragement until I was out of earshot. At which point they presumably returned to whatever they were doing and assuming that I had mental health issues.

Beyond the lock is the Victorian St John's Bridge. William the Conqueror gifted the manor Lechlade to Henry de Ferres and in 1205 Isabella de Ferrers founded the St John the Baptist nunnery which later became a priory. This bridge was built by monks and later the spire was added to the Church in town after Catherine of Aragon took over the manor of Lechlade. It has a fascinating history and, as I have said before, I am fascinated by this sort of thing. This sort of history lesson is the best type of history lesson. I wondered what life was like back in 1205. What did people do? What was fun? I tried to imagine whose footsteps I might be walking in. Did they in turn wonder what the future might be like?

My excitement was boosted further by the appearance up ahead of a series of pillboxes. These simple concrete boxes formed a defence line called Stop Line Red and were built in 1940 to stop Rommel's feared Panzer divisions in the event of a Nazi invasion. Apparently they were never really used, although local bats had taken over this one for nesting.

I had been so pre-occupied by the pillboxes that I had failed to spot a terrifying danger up ahead; a whole field full, I mean full, of cows. Cows seemingly by the million. After yesterday's cow-based scary moment, I was not impressed by this sight. I honestly don't think that I had ever seen so many cows in one place at one time.

My heart beating hard, I slowed practically down to a walking pace and surveyed the scene, dangerously close to a needing-the-toilet-accident. Embarrassingly I was incredibly relieved to see a small boundary wire separating me from them as I got closer. I really don't know why that made me feel safer but it certainly did.

Feeling braver, I ducked into a pillbox to have a quick look around. It had clearly been used for parties judging by the empty beer cans, cigarette butts and empty food packets. The wall has slits in the walls, presumably for observation and firing guns from whilst, I imagine, shouting "shove off Nazi's" (I have a very vivid imagination). On that clear peaceful morning I took a moment to try and imagine what it must have been like in that pillbox in the early 1940s. It must have been incredibly stressful. After the horrors of the Dunkirk evacuation, most people expected to be invaded at anytime so everyone must have been very worried. These soldiers could have been the very first ones to see the German paratroopers and they must have known it could happen at literally any moment. Would they have felt safe in this little concrete hut or out on patrol? After all, if the panzers were outside they would not have much trouble flattening the pillboxes, especially after going through Europe so effectively.

I tipped my baseball cap to those that defended this little island of ours and suddenly my run didn't seem so daunting, even with more cows than I could count outside. Still, at least they were not an invading army. Mind you, I was starting to think that every cow in the world wanted me dead so perhaps they were. Anyway the pillboxes had protected me so they had certainly done their job here.

These thoughts occupied my mind as I passed through Eaton Weir, Kelmscott and Eaton Hastings. After a while I came across Radcott Bridge, parts of which date back to the 12th century. Interestingly it was damaged during a 1387 battle between the Loyalists and Parliamentarians. A battle apparently so fierce and hopeless that Robert de Vere gave it the big legs and escaped to France. Unsurprisingly when news of his fleeing reached his army, they promptly surrendered. Nothing like leading by example is there? It is hard to imagine the chaos of that battle for the vital crossing over the Thames at Radcott Bridge. It's not as hard to imagine how annoyed one would feel, fighting desperately for what one believes in and to stay alive, only to be told that actually the commanding officer has bottled it and run off abroad.

Past Rushey Lock and Weir, a listed structure and one of the last surviving Paddle and Rymer weirs and I soon came across the stunning 18th-century Tadpole Bridge. I'd like to level with you here – I like bridges. And flags too but that isn't relevant right now. I have seen loads of bridges all over the place but this one of the best. Originally it was built to carry the turnpike road to Brampton, is built of stone and consists of one large arch. I stopped to take a photo and take it all in. The quiet of this Oxfordshire stretch of the Thames Path made this a real highlight and, even better, the route crosses the bridge and past the Trout Inn, which made me smile because, for some unknown reason, my brother and I nicknamed our sister Trout from an early age, a slightly unfortunate moniker that still survives to this day.

Following the riverbank, I meandered my way along the trail and soon found myself at Shifford Weir, where I stopped for a photo, a little break and some stretching, as I did at most locks I came across. Just beyond it I came across a curious collection of a farm, cottages and a 19th-century chapel. This is known as Shifford which incredibly would have been a major town 1000 years ago. It always seems incredible to me that a major town can shrink so dramatically. I just don't understand how it can happen. I shall put forward a personal theory though – the town planners of Shifford in roughly AD1013 were pretty awful at their jobs.

The path straightens out here and I could see Newbridge Farm and bridge ahead. I crossed the River Thames here and introduced myself at the Rose Revived, my home for the night. This is a 16th-century inn set quite literally on the Thames Path. So much so that when I left the next morning I ran through their beer garden to do so.

The Rose Revived is a charming place, friendly staff and more restaurant than bar downstairs. My kit had been delivered and was on my bed when I arrived. And so, after a quick warm down, stretch and icing my legs, I washed, changed and headed downstairs where I ate and then returned to my room to rest and watch yet more of the Indian Premier League on television, where I fell a little bit more in love with both the fantastic sport of Twenty Twenty Cricket but also the lady that presented the show.

FLIPPING LOCAL SIGNAGE MAKERS

Early morning Newbridge is handsome, what with the stone of the bridge reflecting in the water. It made for a memorable breakfast location as I ate my porridge, reflecting on the fact that I was now about to be following the same route that the stone quarried near Burford and used to build the Oxford colleges and St Paul's Cathedral had used.

Back on the path, I entered through a kissing gate into a large field where I was impressed by the ground-nesting birds. I love the fact that these gates are called "kissing gates". It is such an innocent name and welcome too, although they can be narrow if you are somewhat big boned. Once upon a time I weighed the best part of 20 stone and I would not have been able to get through a kissing gate at that point in my life. In fact I was so fat in previous times that I once experienced the joy of having 4000 football fans singing at me, accusing me of eating all the pies and of not knowing who my father was, but I digress. This is a beautiful part of the Thames and for a while I forgot about my quest and just enjoyed where I was and what I was doing. Sometimes I just like to run and to forget about the real world because let's be honest, the real world can be a disappointing and upsetting place sometimes. This was one of those moments, a moment where I just drifted onto my own little world and just let everything go for a bit. I kept a close eye out for any cows though.

Those Romans sure got around. The original backpackers, they left several markers along this stretch of river, not least at Bablock Hythe, where they forded and had a ferry crossing for around 1000 years and Roman remains are still evident at Eynsham. Incidentally I really, really like the word "ford". It is so much better than "wade". I think that I shall try and use the term more often.

Heading towards Port Meadow, I passed River Evanlade and Godstow Abbey, which dates from 1139. I was pleased to see a sign that announced Oxford as only being five miles away. I was surprised by this but relieved. It had been a tough day, one of a tough week. Also I had a nagging ache in my left thigh and the sooner I could rest it the better. On and on I ran, fully expecting to see Oxford in all its glory imminently.

But I didn't get to see Oxford in all its glory imminently as, after running for quite a while, I saw yet another sign proclaiming Oxford to be five miles away. My left thigh was increasingly painful and I was tired, so you can well imagine my mood upon this discovery. My parents brought me up well and so I should apologise to the lady walking her dog, approaching from the other direction, who might have been made to feel uncomfortable by the sweating, limping runner that day, who was swearing a little too loudly for a public place and cursing the local sign-making industry.

There was nothing else to do other than carry on, my leg increasingly painful, my limp more obvious and my mood ever darker. Subsequently I was unable to appreciate Port Meadow as much as I would have liked, especially as my day bag then broke and fell to the floor, causing yet another petulant sulk and plenty of swearing again, although thankfully under my breath this time. This was one day I was glad to stop running.

Rachel Davis met me at Oxford train station to drop my bag off. I enjoyed our meeting and really appreciated her help. She gave me a card telling me I was doing really well and that I should be proud of myself. Rachel was also doing a sterling job on spreading the word to attract sponsors and raise awareness of my run. It was all coming together nicely but my leg really was painful and I was very worried about it. After dousing the injured area with cold spray, all I could do was hope for the best when I resumed my run the next day.

From Oxford I took a train to Reading, where I stayed with a friend, Kerrie, who I had met whilst working in America in 2000. She is one of the nicest people you will ever meet and had stocked up on all kinds of foods high in running goodness for me, even going so far as providing a massive bar of chocolate for my next day's efforts. Kerrie agreed to drive me to a local store, where I negotiated a charity discount for a new and much stronger day bag to run with. This was a better evening for me and I enjoyed spending time with someone I knew, which actually would be pretty much the case from now on, assuming all went well. I was very relaxed by the time I hit the sack, fully prepared for a great night's sleep.

Which I didn't get. I just lay there in the darkness, waiting for it to happen. There is nothing, nothing, more annoying than failing to sleep, especially when you actually feel tired. Eventually I just got the hump and that made things worse. My mind was spinning with thoughts of how many more miles to go, my potential leg injury, how stupid would I look if I failed after all this effort and advertising. Would people understand or would they be angry with me?

I felt real pressure on my shoulders that night. It meant that I got no more than three hours' sleep at most which, on top of the mileage already completed, was not good preparation for the next days 23-and-a-quarter mile run.

I rose wearily the next morning and Kerrie drove me into Oxford to resume where I had left off. I had organised today for another good friend, Scwif, to collect my bag and take it on to meet me in Wallingford. All this organisation meant that there was one less thing to worry about, which was very important, especially as I was suffering from a sleep deprivation induced grumpiness. The fact that Scwif had offered to drive from Epsom in Surrey to Reading in Berkshire, collect my bag from Kerrie and then drive on to Wallingford in Oxfordshire to drop it off with me reflects the level of support I was enjoying and also, naturally, what a great bloke he is.

47

I left Osney Bridge expecting to see more people and for the route to be less rural but have to admit that I was wrong. It had rained heavily recently here and it was very boggy indeed. After the initial burst of commuters walking into town, dog walkers, joggers and people out for a stroll, I saw virtually no-one for miles. As ever I kept a keen eye out for cows but so far I remained safe and unchased for the day.

Again though, I was reminded just how beautiful the Thames actually is and how lucky we are to have it in our lives. The path here is very close to the river itself so it was here that I began to be waved at by people on narrow-boats and I could appreciate the speed of a racing eight, out training, complete with bellowing instruction from a cox and sometimes even a separate boat, bellowing instructions on a megaphone. When a racing eight is flying down the river like that it really is a sight to behold, such an art form.

I ran on through Sandford-on-Thames, which was mentioned in the Doomsday book and there past the large and impressive weir. There was a ferry crossing here in the 13th century which presumably means that it is too deep to ford. I just wanted to use that word again.

I had been warned before starting the run that I should be wary of the Sandford Lasher for it had claimed many lives. I didn't know what to think, so was relieved, after further research, to realise that it was the weir at Sandford-on-Thames. If I am honest I had initially misheard the warning and was mildly concerned about meeting the "Sandford Slasher" which, on account of not fancying the idea of being slashed, was something I was keen to not do. Anyone who calls his or her self such a name is not someone I want to meet thank you very much. Anyway the weir at Sandford is highly impressive and I stopped to take the obligatory photo.

After nearly ten miles of very tough running on very wet, boggy ground, I entered Abingdon, an old market town of many years past. I found it a fascinating place to go through and it apparently has evidence of Iron Age, Roman and Saxon times. As I've said before, this was not to be a sightseeing trip; however, I had a job to do and I had to keep on carrying on eastwards. Here in Abingdon people waved from boats and said "hello" or "good morning" as I struggled past. I will certainly also return to Abingdon one day to explore, as it had an interesting feel to it and I am very interested to read since that actually Abingdon claims to be the oldest community occupied settlement in the country. However I will wait until a significant Royal occasion, as the Abingdon Town Council celebrate such an event by hosting a bun fight ceremony in which councillors in full ceremonial robes climb to the top of the County Hall and chuck around 4000 currant buns at the chanting crowds that fill the market place below. It's been going on since the coronation of George II in 1761. Apparently the buns are always baked specially for the occasion and have a crown design on the top. It's a big deal locally and I need to experience this. It is a fantastically crazy and eccentric example of how brilliantly odd this country can be sometimes.

My leg was increasingly sore now and motivation became a real issue. My state of mind was certainly not helped by the realisation that I had only run a little under ten miles at this point and I still had 13.5 miles to go until the day's finishing line in Wallingford. I decided to simply ignore the pain as much as physically possible and so on went the iPod and I took myself to my happy place.

My own personal happy place at this point was the Thames Barrier in that there London which was still so many miles away. In the circumstances I didn't think concentrating on a spot so far away that I had yet to run to was such a great idea so I decided to reflect on what it is that attracted me to running. Was it the health and fitness aspect? To live longer? To lose weight? Or something else? Was it a mixture of all these?

I first started running many years ago because I had a lot of energy and probably drove my parents mad. As I got

49

older I ran because I wanted to be a better footballer. My growth spurt happened as a very young bloke and was a lot earlier than my school chums so I was stronger and more powerful than most, resulting in better performances and times. This of course boosted my self-confidence. In short, running put me in a much better frame of mind, even if I never did become a good footballer.

This will be true of lots of people. Every day of every week of every month of every year of every decade thousands of people take to the streets and run. Be it for fun, health, weight loss or competition, it must be one of the most popular hobbies and sports in the history of the world. Some people are fast, really fast, the likes of Mo Farah, who is capable of running at seemingly impossible speeds and is now a national treasure. Other people run less fast but still very fast. Other people, like me, don't. I've never been a great runner. There I've said it. I always wanted to be, in the same way that I dreamt of captaining the England football team to World Cup glory. I've always trained hard and put the hours in and I suppose really the only thing that stopped me achieving sporting greatness was my utter lack of ability, which is a bit of a shame really.

But the beauty of running is that you don't have to be a great runner. It is one of the greatest activities in the world because it is you against you, a solo race if you will and an activity which does not have to be all about winning medals and standing on a podium. I managed that once, the whole standing on a podium thing, and it was nice but to be honest I have had far better experiences running in events where I finish hours and thousands of places behind the top three. That's me, part of the pack, in running terms nothing special, a plodder. That is not to sound down on myself, it was meant to sound a realistic comment. I know my place and it will never be at the front of a race. And that is OK with me.

What I really enjoy is setting targets and challenges for myself and you are now reading the story of one such project. This whole thing has been a time of great personal development and a time where I have really pushed myself to new levels of effort. I think now that the story is worth telling so, well, I wrote it. And you have picked it up to read which is very nice of you and I am very grateful.

In one other respect I have certainly never been short on guts and am certainly not of a running build. But then again what is the desired build for a recreational runner who likes to challenge himself? If the criteria for such a build is "likes running, likes a pint" then I certainly have got the right build for running. And I have had some great times doing it too, having plenty of adventures running in various places around the world. I run slowly and have subsequently had more time to see places I have run in more detail than the top athletes and I often wonder if they ever take a moment to have a look around from behind their sunglasses as they win yet another race. I mean, they might do, I don't know, but if they don't, they are missing out a bit I think. I have high-fived so many people in running races and spoken to some people that I would never have otherwise. I even once saw a world famous entrepreneur emerging from urinating in the bushes during the London Marathon looking rather sheepish. I didn't high-five him, for very obvious reasons. On another occasion I was overtaken by a Cornish pasty in a push for a marathon finish line which oddly I found quite funny and not as exasperating as you might expect.

So I think there are probably lots of reasons that I run. Firstly I really enjoy it, although every runner will have a day when they feel awful out there and wish they were not doing it at all. In those situations I generally run for a bit and cut the run short. I don't see the point in forcing myself to run for ages if I am not feeling right or really not feeling the love for it. I am well aware that no-one is relying on me to run, it is all about me at these times. There is always tomorrow. Such a relaxed attitude also helps to keep running in perspective. It is not the be all and end all of my life, even with the amount I enjoy it. There are of course other reasons to run, the weight loss is something that is important, especially being the sort of build that nice people refer to as "big boned". And of course I like to get medals for finishing these races too.

And there are the opportunities running has thrown up. I am fortunate enough to have run in events in Australia, France, America, Canada and of course the United Kingdom. I have had a great time seeing new places and I have realised quite a few ambitions along the way but what is really great is that you can just go out and run till your heart is content. Much like cycling or hiking, you don't *have* to have a plan, you can just go out, close the door behind you and go where you like. In a world dominated by technology, be it mobiles, laptops, not to mention the pressures of work, we are still able to leave it all behind us, be totally free and head off exploring if we so wish. Not everyone understands that standpoint but to those people I say try it. It is a big, beautiful, mysterious, ultimately fantastic world out there and it is not, has not, nor will ever be, a waste of time to head out and see some of it. One of the greatest thrills in life sometimes is to get lost. It is true that if we make the effort to put ourselves out there, we can really achieve and experience great things.

And here I was, running along, trying to achieve something I really believed in but my left thigh was bloody killing me. It showed no sign of easing so I stopped often to apply cold spray and to try stretching it. Nothing was really helping and my running style was becoming more and more restricted. I decided to call my Wallingford contact, Jade, and ask her to arrange some ice ahead of my arrival. As ever Jade was delighted to help and that again took some of the pressure off my mind. Now I could just focus on getting to her office.

All of my thinking and focusing on getting the day's run over with meant that I hadn't really taken in my surroundings and so I missed Sutton Courtenay, which dates back to the 5th century and also has a Norman hall dating back to 1192. Appleford church and Clifton Hampden were not really taken in either, although I did manage a brief marvelling at the thatched Barley Mow, a well-known Thames-side pub since 1352. I really wanted to stop there but it really wouldn't have been a great idea. Imagine if my project had failed because I had gotten too comfortable in the pub!

I had regained my senses by the time I neared Little Wittenham, where the world Pooh Sticks Championships are held. I love the fact that there is a World Pooh Sticks Championships and will one day return to see them. What a brilliant, quirky country I live in. I wonder how I can enter the competition. If I did would I be able to say that I was an international, finally? That would tick off another ambition.

Not content with a very sore leg, I gave myself a shock when I saw a sign to Dorchester. I have friends in the Dorset version and, for the briefest of moments, I was convinced that I had taken an almighty wrong turn and spent a few moments amusing myself, thinking of how I would tell people that I had got myself totally lost and had ended up in the south. You have to remember that I was in pain, tired and bored of my own company by this stage. Your mind takes you to some odd comical places to pass the time, believe me. One story that came to mind was District Sports Day in Kingston Upon Thames many years ago now. One lad from our school lined up for the 100 metre hurdles, and false started. He wasn't a regular track and field athlete and didn't realise that a second gun meant to stop. There was quite a large crowd and we all yelled at him to stop but all he could hear was noise, not what we were actually saying so he kept going and, lifted by the support that he thought he was getting from the crowd, actually put in a pretty decent effort. As he cleared the last hurdle, he looked to both sides and, thinking he had won, dipped for the line and then raised his hands to the sky ready to celebrate. It was only then that he saw his fellow competitors still standing on the start line. We all did feel a little sorry for the bloke but I have to say it was pretty funny too and now, for some reason, all these years later, the memory resurfaced in my head and I chuckled my way east, always east, desperately keen to see Wallingford.

The plan for Wallingford was a pretty simple one. I was to meet a young lady there you see. Not like that! Stop sniggering at the back! This young lady answers to the name of Jade and is a colleague of sorts – she works at an advertising company called Alexander Advertising International and so works kind of alongside the office I do. We speak often but had never met. When I saw their postal address by co-incidence, during the planning of this project, I said that I would pop in and say hello.

But the road to Wallingford was not proving to be a fast or indeed a happy one. If my left leg was sore yesterday, it was becoming a real problem today. Every step hurt. Desperate to finish for the day I could hear the office and subsequent pub calling for me. It was like that scene from *Gladiator* where Maximus can see his murdered wife and son but can't quite get to them.

Eventually I came to the fantastic Benson Weir. It is one brilliant weir that, which is a sentence I never thought I'd write. The Thames Trail at this point goes through a field and it was in said field that I finally first spotted the Church Spire of St Peter's which is a redundant Anglican church and is now under the care of the Churches Conservation Trust. It is almost like a "welcome to Wallingford" sign and never have I been so pleased to see a redundant Anglican church before. It put a real spring in my step, metaphorically that is. If I had tried to put a real spring in my step I'd have fallen over.

I love castles and I am fascinated by history, particularly when I am walking in the footsteps of many hundreds of years ago. I think I mentioned it once or twice before? So you can imagine my excitement when I came across the remains of Wallingford Castle. It was established as a Motte and Bailey castle in the 11th century and became what has been described as one of the most powerful royal castles of yesteryear. It faced several sieges but was not captured until the English Civil war when taken by Parliamentary forces on the orders of Oliver Cromwell. Alas it is now just a few remaining walls but it certainly has a presence to it. Standing in the footsteps of part of English history like that provided a fascinating entry into Wallingford.

I headed into the town square where history again hit me right slap bang in the face. Apparently there had been a town here since prehistoric times. In fact it was the lowest point of the Thames, so people were able to ford there. I went into a well-known chain of shops and bought a bottle of water and a chocolate bar as my energy and hydration levels currently left a lot to be desired. I made a call and Jade came down to meet me and then drove me to their office to say hello. Crucially she also bought me a bag of ice for my leg which to this day I am not so sure I paid her back for. Sorry, Jade!

At the office of Alexander Advertising International I met the staff and put faces to names which is always a pleasure, especially when they are as welcoming and pleasant as the staff here. I even found a piece of my work that I had sent over for advertising on Jade's desk ready for the next press run so that was a little surreal. It did look like I did a good job though, fair play to me. I had my photo taken and it was a very nice way to unwind and relax after a tough run. Then the ice finally melted, leaving a puddle under my chair. I just hope that everyone realised it was only water. I felt silly now so we went to the pub.

On Jade's recommendation, we swung by the Boathouse Public House which, as its name implies, is right on the Thames and pretty much the point at which I stopped running for the day a little while earlier. Quite a few rum and Cokes followed and we laughed at the Bar Maid's joke of why the pub's postcode had the letters "BJ" in it. I suspect that was the rum talking.

This was organisation at its finest. My friend Scwif had indeed driven all the way from Epsom in Surrey to

Kerrie's house in Reading and then on to this very pub to first collect and then drop off my kit bag as his support for my edventure, which is why we had asked the postcode of the pub in the first place. It really was a funny joke that the barmaid came up with. Anyway, as he arrived, by chance, so did my friend Alroy, who was picking me up so that I could stay with him and his partner, Linda, for the next three nights. I introduced them all and was pleased that they all seemed to get on. I sat back and reflected that I was joining the world together a little here. I was changing the world a bit in my own small way. I suspect that that was the rum talking.

As much as I was enjoying the rum and Coke, not to mention the valued benefit of not thinking about either my leg or tomorrow's run, I had to be responsible and get up in the morning to begin my noble quest into Tilehurst. And so it was that I reluctantly suggested to Alroy that it was time to go back to his, which is a sentence I had never said to a man before or indeed since.

This was a really beneficial evening for me as, up to now, I had been pretty much thinking about either how far I had run already or how far I had to go. Letting my metaphorical hair down for a couple of hours and just sitting in a pub talking to great people like Scwif, Jade and Alroy was invaluable in the "clearing my head" stakes.

And so onto Wokingham and the spare room of Alroy and Linda. This was yet another example of how well people bought into the project and looked after me. An absolute couple of legends, I was treated like a king. For the next three nights I had my food cooked, my laundry cleaned and Alroy took it upon himself to drive me to my starting point for the day and sometimes back from my finishing point too.

A crucial part of fundraising is making it very easy for people to sponsor you. There is no point in accepting only cash or cheque because times have moved on and other means are available. Alroy is very tech savvy which something that I will never be. We met whilst working for a mobile phone company late last century. Our time working together was basically made up of me having no idea at all what was going on and Alroy helping me. Subsequently I was unsurprised when he suggested something that I had not thought of before – setting up a system through my JustGiving donation page so that people can sponsor me by text. It is pretty simple – all you need to do is set it up so that it is linked to your sponsorship donation account. That way if any money is raised by someone texting in with an amount of their choice, it goes direct to your charity and adds to the amount you have raised. Alroy set it up for me there and then and I in turn logged onto my Facebook page to tell everyone. It created a whole new buzz and meant people could simply pass on the number or donate whilst waiting for the bus or sitting on the toilet if they so wished. Simply put, it made donating easy for people.

The run between Wallingford and Tilehurst started well enough with handshakes and hugs from Alroy, Jade and James, who is the big cheese, the head honcho of Alexanders. Ominously I was limping already and perhaps I should have been more concerned when a huge shooting pain shot down my left thigh as I got out of Alroy's car. I decided to press on and continue, convinced that when my leg warmed up, it would be fine. However I did make the concession to wear a support on said area, to get me started at least.

I have run many miles in my life and have had a lot of terrible runs. However the near 15-mile section into Tilehurst was the worst I have ever felt. Every step really felt like I was being stabbed in the thigh: every step made me feel that there was really no hope and every step made me feel like I wanted to pack this project up there and then.

I was in such discomfort and pain that I didn't take a great deal of notice of my surroundings. All I cared about was my next step. After all, each step eats into what was left. With every step I got closer to Tilehurst, a place that in my mind would be the most beautiful place in the world. All roads lead to Tilehurst.

I struggled on feeling more and more sorry for myself. I was practically going backwards but the one good piece of news was that it was all flat now. I had run into the highest point of the Thames when I arrived in Lechlade don't forget. I really couldn't imagine running hills today. After the beauty of Cholsey Marsh nature reserve, I popped the iPod in and turned the volume up. This might seem a trifle silly what with being alone and injured in a place I didn't know but I needed a distraction and this was my best bet. My friend Richard had cleverly provided me with an iPod full of punk and rock music that I knew. So I attempted to drown out the increasing pain in my leg and began air drumming as I ran and singing loudly, perhaps too loudly for the alarmed looking couple I only saw as I rounded a corner and practically ran into.

Streatley arrived after some stunning views of the Chilterns ahead and a hearty rendition of the superb Oasis track "Slide Away", a song that contains the lyric "give it all you got", a line which seemed incredibly relevant at that point.

Goring-on-Thames is a place I always think should have been the setting for *Dads Army*. I don't know why, but to me it sounds like a lovely place. I bet it wins the local "flower in bloom" competition and has a nice, friendly high street with non-corporate shops and where everyone says hello, please and thank you. I didn't get the chance to explore, so if I am wrong please do not write to tell me. I shall keep the idea alive in my head at least.

I was, despite the pain I was in, still moving, albeit much slower than I had originally planned. I was clearly going to be late to meet my Aunt Vicky at Tilehurst Station so I called her to explain and, she very kindly agreed to put our meeting time back despite already being on her way. All this thinking on the move had been a useful diversion for me and I was starting to think that, with a bit of luck and stubbornness, I might just get through this, especially if the trail stayed even slightly flat.

After making my way past the Goring Bank, I crossed the footbridge over the mill stream and found myself in the Goring Gap.

Arse.

After the last Ice Age, vast amounts of water entered the Thames, the result being that it caused a new route through the chalk at this point. Today it means that there are bloody steep hills to negotiate if, I don't know, you want to run to Tilehurst.

Arse.

This was no laughing matter and my leg was killing me. I had a mobile on me and seriously considered quitting there and then. I could walk back to Goring or Streatley and get a train. No one would mind, I told myself. At least I had tried. I rolled up my running undershirt and looked at my tattoo: "No matter the odds, never give up" it said. I drew to a halt at the bottom of the first big hill to compose myself and get my head together. No. Quitting is not an option.

Looking back on the whole thing, this was a key point. If I quit, I'd be a quitter and would feel like a loser, as I have often felt in life. I had to do this. Gritting my teeth, I pushed on, climbing the enormous feeling hills, urging myself on. I thought of Grandma, the big inspiration for this whole thing. I don't really remember her of course but she had been sick for a long time before she passed away. I bet she didn't just give up, so why the hell should I with a much less serious problem?

Equally my friend Craig. I have always respected him and the dignity and class in which he was conducting himself was very inspiring. He wasn't quitting and also I had his full support. I could not let him, Grandma and the many other people rooting for me down. I also had to do this to prove to myself that I was not a quitter, not a loser and was someone that could achieve something special like this. I had demons to slay. C'mon Ed, get your head together, you have to do this. One foot in front of the other – keep doing that, injuries last for a while, but if you can finish this, the achievement will last forever.

There was far too much riding on this and onwards I ploughed up hill, downhill, up steps, down steps. It is a stunning area and path but I was not able to really take it all in as much as I'd have liked to. I was so psyched up by this time that I felt I could do anything.

Such a pumped-up mental attitude is one thing but all it really meant was that I kept going, not that I got any faster. In fact I was getting slower and so I rang my aunt again to put back our meeting time. I explained what was happening and she was concerned but agreed to meet later.

I got to Mapledurham lock what felt like an age later. I stopped to rest and get the obligatory photo of the lock, and update Aunt Vicky on my progress. I was very bloody late and normally I'd be embarrassed and annoyed about that but today all that mattered was getting there. Getting to Tilehurst Station really was my only focus.

I always tried to not focus on how much further I had to go until the Thames Barrier. At the very attractive Mapledurham lock, however, I couldn't help but notice the sign which reported it was 78-and-a-half miles until the London boundary. Sure, there was no doubt I was making decent progress but I still had a heck of a long way to go. I finally limped into Tilehurst station car park and found Aunt Vicky. Because she had had so much faith in me she was expecting me to be on time, so hadn't brought a book or anything with her. The poor woman must have been bored out of her brain, seeing as how I was three hours late. I'd like to take this opportunity to acknowledge her support and apologise for being so late. Sorry Auntie!

Straight to the pub for a jacket potato with cheese and baked beans (no other filling is appropriate) and the obligatory ice pack was greatly appreciated too. The leg by now had totally seized up and I was having to ask myself some pretty searching questions.

Chief among these questions was whether or not to carry on tomorrow. I didn't want to quit and hated the idea of it, but it had to be considered. The leg didn't hurt now but it was very stiff and I wasn't even able to really walk very well on it, let alone run. After Aunt Vicky dropped me back to Alroy and Linda's, I sat in a hot bath and had a long hard think about it. Sorry about the imagery there, it can't have been very pleasant for you to read, especially if you were eating. Maybe I should offer up a totally different imagery for you. The setting is a lie but it is probably for the best as I've grown up to quite like you, dear reader, and I don't want to leave you with mental health problems.

So here goes.

As I was sitting on the verandah, rocking slowly in my wooden rocking chair, watching my grandchildren play a game of hopscotch, I chewed on a piece of straw as I considered whether or not to run to Henley on Thames, a full twelve-and-three-quarters away. After a great deal of thought I resolved to wait to see how it felt at breakfast as I was too tired to make such a big decision now.

I slept well enough and, sure enough, my breakfast was all ready to go when I walked into the kitchen. I felt like a professional athlete staying at Alroy and Linda's, so brilliant was it. As I ate my porridge I realised that my leg was stiff but not hurting. The omens looked good and I decided to walk a lot more of the Thames today to see how I got on. Obviously the big test would come when I started running. It was one of the shorter days anyway and the weather looked good so I could afford to take my time.

The first thing I realised as I left Tilehurst was that I had made a slight mistake staying with Kerrie a couple of nights back. I should have stayed with her at this point as the trail goes within a few minutes of her house. Another lesson for further edventures had been learnt – do my research better!

The famous Caversham came and went, which sent my historical interests soaring again as I had been told that the Church of St Peter was damaged during the civil war. I think a future holiday or trip might be to tour some of the Civil War battlefields. I think it would be really interesting.

The Kennet and Avon canal is something I am familiar with as it runs into Bath. I used to live about a two-minute walk from said canal and I found it a strangely comforting thought that this stretch of water leads to a place I am so fond of.

A three-and-a-half mile run/walk took ages as I was moving so slowly and awkwardly. Usually when I arrive at a town I was elated because it generally meant that I had finished for the day. Distressingly, my arrival in Reading that day served only as a reminder that I still had about ten miles to go. I stopped to stretch and refuelled, taking the opportunity to take my first pain killers for the day.

This is another beautiful stretch of the river. Moving so slowly and in such great discomfort meant that I tried to take in my surroundings a bit more. And I was impressed by what I took in. After leaving Tilehurst, the railway line above me, the Thames Path is pretty much actually right by the river as it winds past Caversham and Reading. Leaving Reading, which I later discovered actually sits on the Kennet rather than the Thames, I entered Kings Meadow. For most people this would be a welcome relief but I spent the entire time looking anxiously around for cows and working out how I would escape from them if they attacked, despite there being none around. I wouldn't say that I was scared of cows as such but certainly I was apprehensive, so I tried to amuse myself by making up songs about how I enjoy beefburgers.

I stumbled on and found my way through the Wetlands Centre via the paths around the ponds and then the attractive looking Sonning Lock, which reminds me – when I was planning the run I thought that Sonning Lock was a googlewhack. You can imagine my disappointment when I realised it wasn't. Another life ambition still to be realised.

Then it was time to turn left across the 1775 Sonning Bridge. It replaced an earlier wooden bridge and is now controlled by lights and where a pedestrian needs to be careful. Careful I was as I limped across. It had been raining pretty heavily the past few days and today was certainly no exception. As a result I slipped as I returned to the Thames path and did my very sore leg no favours whatsoever and I was again caught out by the locals uttering unfavourable words and phrases when I thought no-one could hear me.

A temporary route took me away from the path and through yet another kissing gate, leading me into a field where I was again convinced I'd be attacked by a herd of cows, onto Lower Shiplake and then another diversion took me over the level crossing at Shiplake Station. When I was a kid we used to travel over a level crossing on our way to meet Dad after he had finished work and I have always been fascinated and excited by them. I used to look both ways and imagine a train coming. Crossing at Shiplake crossing brought back those memories. Incidentally no train ever did come when we were crossing. The powers that be have pretty impressive organisation skills when it comes to that sort of thing.

Surprisingly my leg was now starting to feel a little better and so I upped the pace slightly but slowed down again to marvel at the brilliant miniature railway which is so incredible that it actually has its own miniature station. Seriously, you should see it. It is the best miniature railway I've ever seen and that is a sentence I have never written before. Jogging a little more freely now I continued through the grounds of Park Place and past Marsh Lock. Finally with Henley on Thames agonisingly close, I arrived on Mill Meadows where, after a few minutes, I saw my brother Richard and his wife Emma who incidentally is also my sister-in-law. At this point I knew that the day's running was almost done and I grinned the grin of a cat that was born, bred, educated and still lives in Cheshire at the sight of two such friendly and supportive faces.

Emma had been busy while they waited for me and had, much to my delight, arranged a live on-air interview with Henry Kelly on Radio Berkshire. Mr Kelly and I chatted for a short while and I really enjoyed myself. It was surreal talking into Emma's phone knowing that I was live on the radio. I had never been live before so I just played it simple, answering the questions, remembering not to talk too fast as I often do and, above all, not swearing.

Mum and Dad had arrived by now and the five of us went to the pub where we ate and I iced my leg. You would have thought that I was immune to ice by now. We also found one of those post boxes coloured gold by Royal Mail after the London Olympics. I don't know in whose honour it was painted gold but I had my photo taken next to it. Don't forget that I had been greatly inspired by the London Olympics so it would have been rude to not take the opportunity.

It was a fine afternoon where I again got to forget about the folly of what I was attempting, even temporarily. I was fast learning that, as keen on the project as I was, it was really valuable to kick back and forget about it every now and again. Otherwise it all gets rather heavy psychologically.

Obviously I had had no one to speak to whilst out running and so company was very much appreciated. Before Richard and Emma left to travel back to Surrey, Emma had a further surprise for me. She was by now about four months pregnant and had recently been for a scan. She gave me one of the scan photographs to carry on the rest of my run. Whereas before I had been out by myself, I would now be accompanied by my first nephew or niece. This was another really welcome boost to my mood and, from then on, I would carry said photo with me at all times.

As ever, I left early the next morning, after grateful goodbyes to both Alroy and Linda. My first stop was to be Marlow, eight-and-a-half miles away. My injured leg was still complaining and was very uncomfortable but I felt confident enough to up the pace a little as it had clearly improved recently. Perhaps my body was adjusting to all this. It was raining yet again and so I distracted myself by zoning out and thinking back to yesterday and specifically the scan photo that Emma and Richard had given me. It'll be strange to be an uncle, I reasoned. I wonder what it will be like? Hopefully it might even help me grow up a bit. Only a bit though. I hope that I will be a good uncle. Maybe he or she can learn something from this little run of mine. I mean this whole project is pretty monumental by my standards and not many people I know will ever attempt it, let alone finish it. I can be proud of even reaching this far but if I finish this whole thing, it creates a story for little 'un to hopefully be impressed by in future years. Maybe it will inspire them to have adventures and to try and achieve the ambitions they will naturally have. But I'd like to help teach my niece or nephew as time goes by. I'd especially like to stress to them that it is certainly OK to believe in yourself. I struggled with that for years, for no real apparent reason. There are so many things I regret not achieving because I didn't try. And that is the worst thing – I didn't fail, I just didn't try.

I think that this is partly how I got so motivated to try and run the length of the Thames. I had this incredible and powerful desire to achieve. It was a feeling that I had never experienced before; I wanted this so badly. I had the feeling that, if I could just be successful on this, it would put paid to a large number of personal demons.

I don't want my niece or nephew to ever feel useless and good at nothing. Perhaps because I have been there and experienced that, I can help them avoid it.

With all this thinking, I got to Marlow with no real qualms or concerns. I like the bridge at Marlow, I must say. It is a suspension bridge which, as we all know, is the second best type of bridge, behind a Bascule bridge, the likes of which I very much hoped to see much later in my run.

Marlow Bridge is the only suspension bridge across the non-tidal Thames and was a welcome sight indeed. It was now starting to stop raining and the sun was peeking through the clouds as I repeatedly ran back and forth over the bridge, trying to find where the Thames Trail carried on. Eventually, leaving Marlow behind me, I realised with horror that I still wasn't even half way through the day's running and still had over 14 miles to go. It was time to get a wriggle on.

The journey into Windsor was pretty uneventful at first; I just kept moving forwards in the style of a man who has drunk too much on a night out and suffering from an urgent need to use the toilet. I was, in short, a pretty awful sight. I literally shuffled, and mentally I was increasingly feeling it as I struggled along the trail to the Queen's house. You will remember from earlier I received a good luck letter from Her Majesty's first lady so I idly wondered if perhaps she would be bothered if I popped by on my way to my next pit stop. The letter had said that Queen Elizabeth the Second was very interested in my project and I'm sure that was not made up, so it stood to reason that she would be delighted to receive an unexpected visit from me.

The first large point of reference was Cookham. I have learnt something about a famous Cookham resident you might have heard of called Sir Stanley Spencer who loved his home town so much that he was nicknamed

"Cookham". He was responsible for the painting "The Resurrection" which depicted he and his friends rising from their graves in Cookham Churchyard. I like the painting because to me it symbolises his love for Cookham and his friends. Might it be saying that if your heart resides somewhere you never really leave? Also it hints at ghosts and zombies and that is always enough to keep me happy. I wonder if the nickname 'Epsom' would work.

The run today had again been very tough and I was starting to worry about what it was that I had gotten myself into. Even though my leg was clearly improving, I was still relying on my own stubbornness to help me block the discomfort and I was unable to really run properly with an open a stride as I'd have liked and as a result my pace and progress was very slow indeed.

But every step completed meant that I was a step closer to my goal. If I kept going I would eventually get to Windsor and, today, that was all that mattered. I carried on taking photos of points of interests, signposts and information that I found interesting but this was more to chart my route when I got home and this whole thing was over. I must say that as I ran past the famous Boulters Lock and Maidenhead the thought that the day's run would be over fairly soon, comparatively speaking, was a great comfort.

Often on the run, I found it strange to emerge from hours alone in the solitude of the countryside into the noise of a built-up area and all the people around me. It was a massive contrast and always took me a few minutes to re-adjust. The contrast was clear in Bray, which is famous for its Michelin starred restaurants whereas I drank water from my camel pack and ate jelly beans with a desert of Mars bar.

I've told you how much I enjoyed the London 2012 Olympics and how they inspired me to undertake this challenge. You can therefore appreciate that I was pleased to be running past Dorney Lakes, home of the rowing, flat-water and Slalom canoeing events that fabulous summer.

I'd like to say that I slowed down and took in the moment, to reflect on what I had achieved so far and to say a spiritual thank you, in part to the very site I was now passing. In truth, however, I was shuffling along a pace slower than a snail's anyway. If I had gone any slower I'd have stopped altogether. I had found a comfortable technique to combat the pain in my leg by now but, such was my pace, there was no time for any sentimentality, I just had to keep on moving. I can always go back and see Dorney Lake one day in the future – my Olympic title was to complete the Thames, nothing else. And with every passing step after the lake, my resolve grew and the distance left to run shrank. The Olympic spirit had got me again.

Passing through Boveney Lock (photo duly collected naturally), I passed the Athens Bathing site, a favourite bathing spot for the Eton boys. Opposite Athens is Windsor Racecourse. Now I knew I was getting somewhere, especially when I saw Windsor Castle standing on the hill, an intimidating sight for anyone who had fallen foul of the Royals in previous times, I am sure, but for this particular traveller, a majestic sight. There has been a bridge at Windsor for over 800 years and it was a tremendous thrill to first reach and then cross it. I celebrated by buying cold drinks and yet another chocolate bar after calling my good friend Russell, who had agreed to put me up for the night. Russell and his girlfriend Nicky had only that day returned from their holiday in Antigua and were very jet-lagged but Russell still drove from Chertsey to collect me and then dropped me back again the next morning. This was typical of the sort of support I was enjoying and I was so grateful. I was so tired in the car it was all I could do to stay awake.

I have stayed with Russell and Nicky before. Traditionally such an occasion results in plenty of alcohol and staggering back from the pub via a curry house or kebab shop. It might surprise you however that this was not the case this time. We had a couple of cold beers over dinner, caught up on all our respective news and then due to tiredness (their jetlag, my silly running project), we all slept very well indeed thank you very much. Except that I kept waking up, the result of the most boring repetitive dream in world history, a dream in which all I could see was a river. Nothing happened on this river, I was not boating, swimming or fishing even. It was just a river sitting there, doing nothing. I clearly could not escape my project, even in my slumber.

I CAN'T REALLY BE BOTHERED
TODAY TO BE HONEST

The next day I arose and ate my porridge like a good boy and then Russell drove me back to Windsor where we said our goodbyes and I headed back to the Thames, but only after using surely the world's grandest public toilets ever.

It felt like I had been out in the countryside for months and so today was a day that I imagined I would be really excited about as I was due to cross the boundary into London. And this was the first sign that something wasn't quite right. Usually on this project I got up in the morning, excited by what was ahead of me. Today I awoke feeling very flat, the thought not being so much "bring it on" as "do I really have to?" I felt like I had nothing to give – I was knackered, struggling mentally and my leg was still really hurting. Once I started running, I realised that I had nothing in the tank at all. Where I would usually give myself a motivational talking to when things got tough out there, today I had no desire to do so.

This was going to be a long bloody day.

You won't be surprised to hear that this was psychologically the worst day of the run. I just could not shift the negative thoughts, all of which ate away at my confidence and general well-being. Suddenly little niggles became full-blown muscle tears, the Thames became an enemy and every mile felt like three. What on earth was I doing this for? Was it really worth it? I was hardly saving the world here and no-one would care if I stopped now and just went home. Why would they? I felt as I'd gone as far as I could. Surely this was it? Baron de Coubertin founded the Modern Olympics on the premise that it didn't matter if you won, so long as you tried hard. And I had. In fact I don't think that I had tried as hard at anything as I had on this whole adventure. I'd already won, I'd fought hard to get this far. This was an achievement. I could live with this.

I stopped at a lock to gather my thoughts. I was in really great pain and was out of water. I needed a break and so I sat down on the grass to replenish my water supplies and eat some energy food. I knew that there would probably be days where I was in pain, before I started, but equally I never thought it would be this bad. This was horrible and made me question everything all over again. It is not so bad to quit is it? Where is the shame in trying but failing? At least I tried this time. I will always have that.

In addition, the injury had slowed me down tremendously. I was due at the new Walton Bridge at midday for an interview and picture with a local rag but there was no way that would happen as I was going so slowly. I was pretty annoyed now as everything seemed to get on top of me momentarily. Where had my fighting spirit gone?

I took out my mobile and snapped the regulatory photo and then read the texts I had received so far. I'd had lots of support and I'd really felt like someone there for a bit. It had been a fine edventure and, if this really was the end of it, I had some fine memories to look back on. I sat there, looking out over the water, wondering what to do when, suddenly my phone was bleeping; I was a part-time youth worker at this time in my life and my boss Lesley was wanting to come say hello and had got in touch to say that she would run with me for a while as I arrived at the new Walton Bridge. Then another bleep-bleep, this time an answerphone message from my other work colleagues to say that they would be at the same bridge to cheer me on at about the same time. They had all agreed to take their lunch break at the same time to come say hello. That was nice of them, Lesley too. It would be like having a welcoming party.

Motivation restored, I would run on.

I carried on, one leg working very well, the other one improving but screaming blue murder every time it touched the floor, although a large part of that was probably in my head, looking back on it.

I am fascinated by the Magna Carta, signed by King John in 1215 and which accepted the Barons' demands and also liberated the country from the Power of Absolute Monarchy. And it happened here, somewhere in the area in which I now ran. It is such a quiet area and yet has such an important place in world history. I had always intended visiting the memorial at this point, but I had to keep focused on the job in hand. I had to get to Kingston Upon Thames today and it was still a very long way away.

A while later Staines came into view. Now known as "Staines Upon Thames", because to add "Upon Thames" clearly makes a massive difference, it has been a river crossing point since Roman times (did they ford?) and apparently the Barons gathered here in 1215 before meeting King John to sign some document or other. I was also interested to learn that Staines was a horse-change site when news was being delivered about Horatio Nelson's death in 1805 at the Battle of Trafalgar.

On and on I ran and soon ran under the frustrating Chertsey Bridge. I say "frustrating" because I realised at this point that it really cannot be too far to Russell and Nicky's place. Still it felt like progress to be here as, through the open space in Laleham Park, I sensed that things were getting bigger – the noise of the cars, the places I was running past.

This was a unique point in the run as I was forced to take a ferry crossing to the other bank to continue along the trail. I am a big child really and so it was exciting to ring the bell and wait for the very friendly chap to come out and take me across. It cost me £2 and was a great novelty experience. Even better was his reaction when I explained what I was doing and how far I was attempting to run. I think that he thought me very silly.

The last time I had visited this area was to watch my friend Tony launch his home-made boat, Seriously he built his own boat and it was named the *Mental Pencil*; I had gone out in it for a paddle and nearly capsized it when getting in, such is the level of my balance and athleticism. On this visit, thanks to my leg which, as I have mentioned, was not on very good form at all, I looked rather ungainly as I tried to disembark the ferry boat and, of course, this was how and when my work colleagues Rikki, Dave, Steve and Peter found me. Cleary it was not part of my destiny to get in and out of boats here. We caught up for a while at Walton Bridge and many photos were taken, particularly after Lesley had found us. I had been so delayed that my pre-arranged photo and interview with a local journalist had been missed. That was a shame and I was sorry about that as it is always nice to have a picture of your mug in the local paper but I was still in the game at this point and that is what mattered.

After leaving the edventure fan club, I plugged my iPod in and rocked out at my own personal rock and roll festival as I staggered past a couple of pubs, both of which looked very inviting, Elmbridge leisure centre and then Sunbury Weir. As I got closer and closer to the London boundary, my iPod played "Rock 'n' Roll Star" by Oasis which summed up how I was now starting to feel. I have always loved the track and so I played it on repeat more than a few times. My motivation and mood was improving rapidly as I passed Molesey Lock and a massive smile spread across my face as I finally crossed the London boundary, otherwise known as Hampton Court Bridge. After nearly 150 miles up hill, down hill, through fields, up and down a tree, over stiles and along towpaths, all with a very sore leg, I was finally back in the capital. And it felt brilliant.

I celebrated by buying a chocolate bar and can of Coke opposite Hampton Court Station. I was a very happy man now. I wanted to go for a celebratory beer but I knew that there was one last thing to do before my day's running was over. When I designed this run I asked around to see if anyone wanted to join me for a bit. Plenty of people said that they would and didn't, but my friend Dan kept to his word and joined me at the bridge to run alongside me into Kingston Upon Thames. However he only did that after changing on Hampton Court Bridge out of his work clothes into his running gear. I can only apologise to anyone who was there that day. I was also to be joined by my good friend Sam, who cycled over after finishing work and would also accompany me on this stage of the journey. With Sam cycling on my left and Dan running on my right, it was strange to have company for the three-and-a-half miles' jog and I kept them entertained with some what I thought were hilarious thoughts and anecdotes from my efforts so far. Then again what I find hilarious is often not what other people think even remotely amusing, so perhaps they were just being kind to the poor fool doing all this running.

At one stage Dan seemed to be struggling with the pace, although I think that he was putting it on for comedy effect but which, of course, meant that we teased him for it, in a good-natured way obviously. I was really starting to relax and the sight of Kingston relaxed me further. At Kingston Bridge my sister Lucy, brother Richard, sister-in-law Emma, friend Tony and Sam's girlfriend Sally along with their daughters Chloe and Daisy were waiting for me. Such was the excitement felt by the welcoming party that my brother filmed a complete stranger running towards him, thinking it was me. God knows what the chap thought as he had a bunch of strangers pointing a camcorder at him and shouting encouragement, all the while calling him Ed. It was probably quite a surreal moment for him I imagine. Unless he was named Ed, then less so as presumably he would be used to people addressing him as such.

Eventually the three of us appeared and Emma ran up to high-five me before Sam and Dan left me to continue this last bit by myself which was a nice touch, particularly as those present clapped me and shouted encouragement, no doubt relieved that this time that they had the right runner. You would also think that my brother, being by now in his mid-thirties, would know what I look like, added to the fact that he was expecting three runners not one but there you go. Finally, after the regulation photos we headed to The Ram where Dan's then girlfriend Lucy joined us. She amused me by quoting Alan Partridge at every available opportunity, in the same way that my friends Alroy and Sam do. Anyway we all had a pint or two and a bite to eat before I headed back to Sam and Sally's where I was to stay for the night, waking up in the living room the next morning to the sound of a very young Chloe trying to understand why I would be running all day and why I would want to, sentiments that at times I would have to agree with to be honest.

I was now over the London boundary and therefore it was time to make two changes – I switched the guide-book I was using from *Thames Path in the Country* to *Thames Path in London*. I had never been excited to swap books before. And I also swapped my off-road running shoes for a pair of more-suitable-for-road-running-ones too.

I might now be in London but I still had another 40 miles to go until I reached the Thames Barrier. Suddenly motivation was not such an issue anymore. It had been an extremely tough day, one that pushed my mental strength to its capacity. I slept that night in the knowledge that better days were ahead.

Kingston Upon Thames is the nearest to a hometown I had on this journey. I hail from nearby and spent many a happy hour as a young man sampling the delights of its nightlife. In fact one of the very first pubs I ever regularly used was The Ram, so it had seemed appropriate that I visit there to celebrate the completion of that particular leg of my run. It was nice to add another reason for going there along with A Level results, dates or just a night out with the lads. I mused upon this as I walked back through Kingston the next morning and rejoined the Thames Path. It's funny how things change in life – when I was a young man, there were certainly times when I would not have gone for a run due to the amount of alcohol I had consumed the night before in this very town. Now it was a convenient stopping point for the run of my life.

This is another very nice stretch of the Thames and it was a pleasant enough morning. I had left early enough and so I had plenty of time ahead of me. So I jogged slowly, taking in the sights, up past Thames Young Mariners, where I once earned my one star canoeing badge and up to Teddington, the lock just behind it. A quick use of the facilities here and a photo (of the lock, not me using the toilet) and on I pushed, reflecting in the morning sunshine how well the run was coming along. I was still limping but my body had adapted a bit by now to cope with it all and, much more currently relevant, even the Thames had changed to a tidal river. All those miles behind me were now part of the "old" Thames so far as I was concerned. Things were really developing now and I was really starting to think that I might actually do this after all.

I had been warned before this part of the run that this section of the Thames Path is prone to flooding at high tide and to check the tide times before setting off. You can guess what I had forgotten to do, so I ran a little into the unknown at this point. All was well however, right up until my left foot started to hurt. I had not had this before and it was a really piercing pain. Had I suffered some kind of stress fracture? It felt like agony, like a reasonably large stone had somehow penetrated my shoe and was attacking my foot.

I had stopped at a bench to rest and investigate, I emptied my left shoe of a large stone that had somehow penetrated my shoe and was making itself busy by attacking my foot and then carried on, pain free, and confident that, if that was the extent of today's problems, I was going to do OK. Shortly after, I had a chuckle to myself as I remembered the obese man near Kingston earlier who, thinking he was alone, had stopped to relieve himself in a bush and was mightily shocked and alarmed by my sweaty appearance coming around the corner. If I had only had the presence of mind to shout "boo" it would have been better but, as it was, if I had done that, I think the fellow would have relieved himself in a whole other way.

Eel Pie Island passed on my left after I had negotiated Ham Lands (no cows attacked me here either. I had been worried) and suddenly the Star and Garter home on Richmond Hill was in view and the Marble Hill House, built as country retreat for one Henrietta Howard, mistress of King George 2nd. Both are striking buildings, the latter reminding me a little of the famous White House in Washington DC.

The oldest surviving bridge over the Thames is at Richmond and was opened in 1777. I've said before that I like bridges and this was a bit of a surprising highlight of the Thames. It is Grade 1 listed and even has a Victorian gas lamp post on it which has been converted to electric light. The whole bridge has a real class about it and I don't mind saying so. You are thinking it anyway, let's be honest.

I later found out that Richmond Lock and Weir has an interesting story. In 1832 the old London Bridge (including its 19 piers and protective palisades) was demolished. Without the protection afforded by the bridge, the tides on the River Thames rose and fell far more rapidly than they had ever done. Incredibly this meant that for a long time, the Thames here was really no more than a stream running through mud. It is so hard to imagine now but many people campaigned for a long time to build a half-lock and weir downstream of Richmond Bridge. This ultimately meant that the river was restored to its former beauty and condition. It was opened by the future King George V in 1894. I think that my grandad lined the route at his coronation.

Good old Grandad. I'm in his neck of the woods now. I bet that he would think me crazy for doing this but he would be really proud too. He took quite an interest in my running and was delighted when I took around my London

Marathon medal and finishers T-shirt to show him in 2005. I can never be proved right of course but I am very sure that, had things been different, he'd have come out to meet me on the Thames path around here somewhere. I bet we'd have stopped for a pint too, just like so many other times.

As would Grandma of course. She was a London girl, apart from during the war when she did her bit whilst based in Guildford. Grandad once told me that somehow one weekend he got leave and wanted to get Grandma away from the hell of the blitz. They went to Bath... and the very same weekend the Luftwaffe decided to not hit London quite as hard and attack other cities such as Bath for a change. They couldn't believe it when the air raid siren went. I bet they had the right hump, although I recall Grandad laughing a little as he told me that story.

Thoughts like these occupied my mind as I left Richmond and passed the Grand Union Canal, Brentford and finally Kew Gardens before arriving at Kew Bridge. I wished that I could have stopped to take in the sights but as ever I knew that I had to push on for a while yet as I had people waiting for me near Hammersmith Bridge, the next big personal milestone.

There have been plenty of times on this run that I have come across something that I didn't have time to explore and here was another. As I plodded along, I noticed to my left a small island, which turned out to be called Oliver's Island. Rumour has it that Oliver Cromwell hid on this island from the Royalist troops during the English Civil War and held military meetings in the adjacent Bulls Head public house. I didn't know all this at the time, other than what was in my guidebook but what a story! Mental note was made yet again to make a return visit, along with so many other places. I was fast realising just how vital the River Thames was, is and always has been. It is like a big floating history book and I was starting to gain a deep affection for it. I also love the idea that Cromwell planned his civil war tactics in the pub. This country has a deeply held affection for a public house and it is quite heartening to think that even then it was seen as somewhere safe and welcoming. I can't even begin to imagine the security. How would that have worked? If the Police have trouble these days with knives and violence at kicking-out time, they would have had an absolute nightmare with that lot when the bell rang.

After passing Chiswick Bridge I was on a very famous stretch of the river indeed – the course of the famous University boat race between Oxford and Cambridge, which was first raced in 1829, making it one of the oldest sporting contests in the world. OK, so I was running the route from finish to start but, hey, I was still running it. This famous race finishes opposite the Ship Pub, which must surely mean that it rakes in an absolute fortune on boat race day. You can't make for a much better spot, especially if it is a close race. How can they possibly go wrong?!

I was increasingly excited at this point as this part of the river is possibly the part that I go furthest back on. When I was a young lad, my dad worked in Hammersmith and as a treat during school holidays, Mum used to bring me, my brother and sister up to meet him when he finished for the day. I recall we took the number 72 bus up which had several important responsibilities. It was always, always, a double-decker bus and it was the start of the route, so Mum used to let me and Richard go charging upstairs while she paid so that we could claim the best seats in the house. It was essential to us that we always got the front right upstairs seats. This was because that side had one of those mirrors so that the driver could see what was happening on the top deck and what the passengers were up to. We used to dare each other to look down it. We were right adventurous like that. Good times.

I got to Hammersmith Bridge and crossed over onto the north bank, where I briefly turned back on myself for half a minute or so until I arrived at the Blue Anchor pub, which I am told features as part of the classic television show *Minder*. Here I met Dad, my sister Lucy and family friends Emma and Nikki. A couple of very nice drinks ensued and I iced my leg whilst I told everyone what had been happening and where I had been. It all now started to feel a little surreal, reflecting on what I had done and what I still had to do. It really did feel that I had already achieved so much and this made me feel all warm and fuzzy inside. If I felt like this now, how on earth would I feel if I actually made it to the Thames Barrier?

My run for today was still not complete and I had to head off after a while. My next stop was a bit of a unique element to the whole run – a lap of the pitch at Craven Cottage, the home of Fulham Football Club. When I was a young lad I was watched by Fulham in a match. I was absolutely hopeless, was unfit, couldn't pass, shoot, tackle or head a ball. On top that I scored 5 own goals and kept playing their striker onside because I didn't understand the offside rule. I had a terrible game. Anyway they offered me a place.

Now running east again, I jogged on to meet my contacts Ceri and Carmelo. Both of which, as things turned out, were unavailable at the last minute but that's OK because Sarah and Caroline on reception had been well briefed and were very welcoming. Dominic the security guard was called who escorted me pitch side and patiently waited and watched with Dad, Lucy, Emma and Richard who had met me there. They laughed politely as I posed for photos and shot videos of me clapping an imaginary crowd before running down the players' tunnel. And then my brother interviewed me about the run, on camcorder, in the same place that the footballers fulfil their media commitments after a match. It was an interview where I tried to throw in as many football cliché responses as possible, right down to saying how amazing the edventure fans are for supporting me so enthusiastically. It was a really nice, silly, light-hearted moment and I greatly enjoyed myself.

Equally enjoyable was the food that Ceri had very thoughtfully organised for me in the "Haynes Café" there, once I had finished inside the ground. After so much exercise, some sustenance was greatly appreciated. Outside this café is a statue of former Fulham and England captain Johnny Haynes which is actually a very fine sculpture indeed but one that got me thinking again. When England won the World Cup in 1966 the ever present Right Back and Vice Captain was George Cohen, whose club side was Fulham and he played his entire career here at Craven Cottage, apart from away games obviously, I am sure he played a few of those. So they have a World Cup winner here. Why has he not got a statue? Surely he deserves one after a career as a one-club man here and winning football's greatest prize? When you think that realistically England are unlikely to win it again anytime soon and that it is now nearly 50 years since Bobby Moore lifted the Jules Rimet trophy, has there ever been a more appropriate time to erect such a memorial to a fine achievement? I resolved privately to contact the club when all this was finished to see what they thought.

Finally the day's running was over, once I had run the mile or so from the stadium to Putney Bridge. I mentioned at the start of this story that I used to visit Grandma weekly with Mum when I was in a pram and sometimes we used to walk here, right here. In fact I think that there is a photo of little old me in my pram on this very path. This whole area has been a big part of my life since I was born and I feel comfortable and at home here. I passed to the right of St Mary's church, which has been there for hundreds of years and was a very picturesque way to finish the run. Just so I would always know where I had touched the bridge, I used the plaque commemorating Sir Joseph Bazalgette, who had built this bridge in 1886... but only after I had done a theatrical sprint finish, whooping and hollering for the benefit of the video camera with Richard and Emma shouting Rocky quotes at me along with a running commentary.

It was only as I finished I realised that there was a chap sitting reading on the bench nearby, looking at me like I was the biggest freak alive. I tried explaining that I was running the whole length of the river for charity but he sort of shrugged his shoulders and went back to reading. I admit it, my ego took a bit of a blow at that point. How could he not be impressed by what I was attempting? And then I realised that I was being a bit arrogant so I took a step back and told myself off for not being very cool.

That evening's base camp was in Putney with a friend of mine, Natalie, who for some unbeknown reason I have always called Natalia and who lives with her sister Lucy and who had very kindly allowed me to sleep on a camp bed in their front room. This was a very pleasant evening, where we went out and bought some carbohydrate-based food and then sat around talking. Once again I was enjoying hanging out with lovely people. I really think that the people I encountered on this trip was one of the biggest highlights of it all. I am so lucky to know the people I know.

There was a real single-minded determination in my mind to finish this thing now. I was still limping and my leg still really hurt but I knew that I was very close to completing the river and I was determined to do so. I refused to think that I was certainly going to do it as I knew that I had to stay in the here and now and not get too carried away, but that said I was becoming increasingly confident.

The next morning I was up bright and early to head to a part of London that I knew well and was immensely looking forward to – Tower Bridge. Sticking to the north bank, this bit of the Thames Path is a bit of a maze but well signposted, guiding you around Hurlingham Park and back to the Thames via Broomhouse Lane and Carnwath Road in no time at all. I had made it to Wandsworth Bridge and I stopped to marvel at how many people there were all of a sudden. I had forgotten that it was a weekday, every day was a day on leave for me at the minute and I had forgotten that actually the rest of the world was still carrying on, and grumpy looking people were all heading off to do their thing. I felt a little unsettled in a way as I had gotten used to being alone for so many days. Here in London there were sirens, car horns, people on phones and nannies taking children to school, everything seemed to be happening. I wondered at this point whether I would have been better off running the Thames the other way round, so that I could escape the city noise and finish with the peace and quiet of the country. Mind you, that would have meant being chased up a tree by three angry cows on the very last day of the run which might not have been so funny, especially if I still had a bad leg and couldn't actually climb a tree. It is a sobering thought.

After Wandsworth Bridge, the north bank of the Thames Path travels directly alongside the Thames itself, under the Battersea railway bridge (or to use its correct name "Cremorne bridge") and past Chelsea harbour, where I had a quick look for Roman Ambramovich but he was not about it seemed. I am not entirely sure what I expected to find, it is not as if he would be there cleaning his boat and emptying the chemical toilet after all. From this side of the river you can see a heliport which reminded me of one of my great ambitions in life, to fly in a helicopter. Ever since I was a child, a child that used to love watching *Airwolf* (a helicopter that used to have a silent mode so that it could sneak up on unsuspecting bad guys. I kid you not), I have always wanted to go up in one. I guess it is the same train of thought that means every child my age wanted a car that could talk or have a "turbo boost" mode, or in the *Dukes of Hazzard* where those good ol' boys kept driving fast and jumping over things. They didn't even use the car doors, preferring to use the window instead. Even now, when I am driving and overtake people, I whistle the famous horn sound that the Dukes of Hazzard car made. I must be great company to drive with; I think I am desperately trying to cling onto my youth. Dad used to watch these shows with us, the *A-Team* too, but he made an extra special effort to watch *the Dukes of Hazzard* with us. I don't know why exactly but I think it was the car. Yes, that must have been it.

I soon passed the Lots Road Power Station, which to be honest, I was pretty ignorant about but I looked it up later and found it had supplied the electricity to the London Underground as recently as 2002 which really made it, in my eyes, one of the most important buildings in London.

They love a blue plaque in these parts – plaques remembering Sylvia Pankhurst (suffragette and anti fascist), Hilaire Belloc (satirist) and Marc Brunel (engineer) are all placed in the area. I like the blue plaque idea I must say. It is nice to remember people that made a difference to the world before we came along. I would love it if one day a blue plaque was placed on my childhood home front wall. I say that I'd love it but in reality I probably wouldn't know, but it is a nice idea anyway.

I crossed the Thames at Battersea Bridge after admiring the fine statue of the painter Whistler. Now on the south bank, my excitement was starting to build as I got closer to London "proper". This was London, where I fully intended finishing running the famous River Thames and then running the city's famous marathon. I'd had the feeling before but now, barring things going really wrong, surely I'd make it. Passing Battersea Park was rather nostalgic for me as it was here that I had trained and competed for a running club; memories of promotions, team mates, meeting international standard runners and even of winning medals came flooding back. I transferred to this team because the events, coaching and facilities were of a much higher standard and as a result this was a golden running time for me, a time where I really improved and, looking back, sadly in terms of performances and results, a time during which I peaked. In 1988 I qualified to represent Epsom and Ewell at the County cross-country championships after finishing eighth in the borough race on Epsom Downs. I finished 58th and really enjoyed it: I won two out of three 800-metre sports day events and also finally achieved my ambition of being selected to run in the district sports championship at Kingsmeadow, where I ran the 1500 metres. In the years before I was selected for the District Sports team I used to watch the team practise, desperate to be out there running with them. I resolved to make it, and make it onto the team I did. I still take great pride in that. And I put in a lot of training hours to achieve these things near here, on that track in Battersea Park.

In 1991, I was part of the 4x400 metre relay team and we had dominated pretty much all of our races, smashing club records all over the place as the team won two consecutive promotions and I spent my last year as a young athlete in the premier league. I had by now long realised that I was never going to be a great runner and was being pulled along time-wise by the rest of the team. I had already peaked and was not going to get any faster. We had such a great atmosphere amongst the team and we all got on well but I was jealous of their talent and annoyed by the fact that most didn't seem interested in trying to take that ability as far as they could. They all won stacks of awards and medals and I was just making up the numbers, desperate to get my hands on a AAA medal. I knew that individually I didn't have the ability to get one and that the relay was my only hope to earn something I so desperately wanted. I was also beginning to accept that my time was almost up as I was now being overtaken by other athletes and would probably be dropped from the relay team soon. It was pretty obvious that the 1991 AAA relay championship in Kingston Upon Thames was my best and last hope.

Each year, after the busy track and field season had wound down, we used to get September off. God knows why we did that year because that's when the championships were held. We had been on a family holiday and had flown back from Canada only two days before. I was not on great form and I was very nervous indeed. I don't remember much about the race itself other than it rained a bit and that a lot of people seemed to be watching. I do know that I ran the slowest time of the four of us and we finished third, ensuring I got my bronze medal. We were capable of at least silver and probably would have got it if Coach hadn't given us that month off. Anyway I was elated and remember shouting "I want my medal" at no-one in particular. Alas we didn't get to go on a podium, it was just a chap on the side of the track by the event organiser's office giving out medals from a box. It didn't detract from my excitement though. I still have the medal and am still very proud of it.

I was still loving the art of running itself but increasingly running track and field was becoming a chore, especially as my friends had discovered the pub by now and by this time my relationships with the other lads on the team had broken down and I was not so much a part of the team. We were all growing apart and I was beginning to feel quite alone. I have never been 'cool' but suddenly everyone around me was. On the team coach these days I generally sat alone. One of the most bittersweet days of my life was the day that I won the B string triple jump at a premier league meet. I was so proud that I had finally done something worth talking about but not one person congratulated me from the team or cheered when it was announced over the PA system. Everyone must have known how hard I worked and, after all, I had just won the team some points but warming down alone and congratulating myself because no-one else did, was a very flat moment. Everyone around me was winning medals in the big meets and I was left watching them, jealous, pleased for them but frustrated that I was never going to achieve that level.

My "competitive" track and field days came to an end shortly afterwards. I picked up a bit of an injury and told Coach that I needed to rest it. I never spoke to him again. He didn't call me and I took it as a sign that it was all over. By this time I was tired of all the training and needed a break mentally. Anyway I had discovered a new love and her name was the King William pub in Ewell Village.

Over the next few years I lost all interest in running track and training hard. I still ran occasionally and every now and again tried to get fit but I loved being in the pub, having a laugh. I got very, very fat and really quite lazy. This can happen when you drink too much and it certainly did to me.

So here I felt as though a huge weight was being lifted off my shoulders as I jogged on by. For so many years I had been frustrated and perhaps even a little bitter that my running ambitions had not materialised. Yet if I could just keep going to the Thames Barrier, I would achieve something that I could be so very proud of. I felt as though I was getting my own back and letting go of something. I was never going to be an Olympian, I know that, but I deserved more than being simply ignored. Sport for young people shouldn't be just about winning medals. After all, if the top eight 100-metre runners in the world lined up and raced, one of them would still come last. I really believe that, whilst it is important to nurture prospective gold medal winners, the slower runners also help to make the sport as brilliant as it is. Look at almost any large marathon – thousands of people still cheer the ones who finish at the back of the field just as loudly as they do for the winners.

So with these thoughts in mind, my demons now firmly in my past, I carried on, increasingly proud of myself. It was a shame though that I reached Albert Bridge in daylight hours as it is famous for being illuminated, so I resolved to one day return and see it for myself. With all these return trips, I will be one busy man.

I was enjoying being by the water, especially now that I was really feeling that I was getting somewhere, so I was disappointed when the Thames Path was forced away from the river itself for a little while after Chelsea Bridge. It did give me the chance to run through commuters and people who had the grump on again though. Again, I had forgotten about the real world and suddenly I was forced to be careful of people on their mobiles and even one lady who was walking along whilst reading a book. I have seen this before and it never fails to amaze me: how does anyone ever think that this a safe and clever idea? It has to be dangerous and really does do my head in.

After being directed along Nine Elms Lane, I rejoined the river at Vauxhall Bridge and was now only four miles from Tower Bridge.

I was always going to run on this part of the Thames along the South Bank. I love the atmosphere and the buzz of the crowds sightseeing at a truly iconic spot. Since I was a young boy I have always loved the view of the Houses of Parliament and Big Ben. And here it is now, approaching on my left as I made my way along the Albert Embankment and past the naked Old Father Thames depiction. It was rather a famous London day today as it was the funeral of Margaret Thatcher. Love her or hate her, she can certainly draw a crowd and she had certainly done that so I was keen to not hang around as I didn't want to be caught up with thousands of people. As it turns out, however, anyone protesting or paying their respects were on the other side of the river so my decision to run the South Bank turned out to be an excellent one. As a consequence I had plenty of space to run in.

I really love this part of London and one the reasons is that there are some quirky things to discover – did you know for example that the pineapples at either end of Lambeth Bridge are a nod to one John Tradescant who grew the first British pineapple. Apparently his dad was a gardener to Charles I, and the family are buried in St Mary's here. I guess that if you cannot have a statue after you have gone, a piece of fruit is a decent compromise.

Big Ben chimed the hour as I approached Westminster Bridge which seemed appropriate. Now I was in a very good mood indeed so I stopped and asked a tourist to take my photo in front of the Houses of Parliament, something which seemed to confuse her judging by the amount of time it took her. For some reason I felt compelled to apologise to her for this, which is a very London thing to do. Whoever said that people in the capital are impolite eh?

I went on the London Eye once and it was ace. I took a friend of mine who was in town briefly. It is such a great addition to the capital and this was proven by the incredibly long queue to get on it. I had to slow down, rightly, to dodge my way through them, which gave me some time to appreciate both the London Aquarium and the London Dungeon. I'll have to return one day to see them both, although I think that I will wait until my niece or nephew is old enough and so that, if I am scared, I can say that I'm being a responsible uncle and get him or her out of there. I refer to the dungeon of course, I doubt that the aquarium would scare me, although I wouldn't want to get too close to a crocodile. If I did I certainly wouldn't smile at it.

I have seen many statues in London but I am quite amazed that Sir Joseph Bazalgette does not seem to have one. Why is this? It seems rather unfair? I am not sure I knew anything about him before embarking on this project but even a casual look into his life shows what a remarkable man he seems to have been. He was the Chief Engineer of London's Metropolitan Board of Works who created a sewer network for central London which resulted in relieving the city of cholera epidemics and subsequently began the cleansing of the River Thames. Knighted in 1875, elected President of the Institution of Civil Engineers in 1883, he also designed bridges of such note as Maidstone, Albert, Putney and Hammersmith. In 1897 he produced plans for the Blackwall tunnel and proposed plans for what later became Tower Bridge.

He does have a Greater London Council blue plaque in St John's Wood and a formal monument on the riverside of the Victoria Embankment but surely a statue somewhere in the heart of London would be appropriate? Everywhere you look in London it seems that his legacy smacks you in the face and maybe ultimately that's the best type of memorial but I do think that the capital should remember such a London hero. I might write to my local Member of Parliament and ask what he thinks. Tell you what, if this story ever gets published, I'll investigate starting a campaign.

I'm on familiar ground now as I plod my way along the South Bank. I was aware of what was happening on the other side of the river and of whistles and far-off noise but thankfully there was no chance of being caught up in any crowds. I was happily taking in the sights of the capital when a sudden noise shook me to the core. I had not been able to follow the day's timetable so to speak so didn't really know what to expect, other than the presumed crowds. So the ensuing cannon fire in tribute to Mrs Thatcher absolutely made me jump. It was, I believe, highly fortunate that there were so few people around me at this point as I think I uttered several choice words and words which enquired whether God was being serious or not. Whatever my thoughts on Margaret Thatcher I will always remember her funeral as the one that scared the crap out of me.

My breathing and heart rate settled as I approached my day's finish line at Tower Bridge. I took my photos and had a chat with a Polish television crew, who gave me a round of applause when I told them what I was up to. I really hoped that they would interview me and I'd end up on television in Poland, but no such luck. It would have been nice to enter the consciousness of the Polish people and there are not many boys from Surrey that could say they have achieved that. I still think that it was a missed opportunity.

Tower Bridge is the greatest bridge in the world. That is a big statement isn't it? But I stand by it. I love how imposing yet comfortable it looks on London's skyline. There might be bigger and more efficient bridges but surely none grander. This was one of the sights I was most looking forward to. I have seen it before of course but I never tire of it. I must have a million photos of it at home as I always seem to take a few when I am there. I just cannot get enough of it. Which probably makes me weird but there you go, it is a harmless enough obsession after all. When I got there that day, I walked over it and they were starting to set up for the Virgin London Marathon, which brought things home a bit. It was all very well being about thirteen miles away from the Thames Barrier but actually I still had a full marathon to run after that. Any vague ideas that this thing would now be easy to complete were instantly erased as I realised that actually I still had about 40 miles to run in total. For now though I was finished on the Thames for the day and had quite a few hours to kill, so I filled it by popping over to the London Marathon Expo at Docklands to meet some of the ladies from the British Heart Foundation and collect my race number for Sunday's marathon.

They have a wall at the Expo where runners are encouraged to leave whatever messages they want to. When I was there the messages already left said things like "what am I doing?" or "scared!" There were also some motivational messages left for co-runners too; "you're ready" or "believe" and the like. I opted for a message for a very special person, the reason that I am doing all this: "Yo Grandma! This one's for you". And then something about how I always said I would do this for her and the British Heart Foundation. It wasn't planned and not something I ever expected to write but it all flowed naturally and felt right so I carried on and it ended up saying what it says. The words are, I think, a bit Rocky Balboa like, but that is fine by me as he is one of my very favourite film characters. I can quote large parts of his films and I often refer to his films when training. I even once went to Philadelphia just to run the famous steps. It was a couple of days after I had completed the New York City marathon and to be honest I think it nearly killed me running up them due to the stiffness in my legs. Then I took a walk around the Expo, collected my race number and runner's pack containing all the information I would need for the big day and then had a nice long chat with the

British Heart Foundation Heart Runners team. We discussed what I was up to and they seemed genuinely interested and grateful for my efforts.

I couldn't stay too long as I had a very important appointment with my good friend Craig and his wife Kate. Craig was in London for a medical appointment and, truth be told, I had actually planned this part of my run to start much earlier than usual and with great cunning so that I can be in town on this day and able to say hello. It was a very pleasant couple of hours talking and catching up. If I am honest, Craig's nurse caught my eye a little too but that is another story. Actually, there is no other story there at all. All that happened was that I thought her attractive, went red, stammered a little and she stayed away from me after that. Anyway I really enjoyed spending time with these two very lovely people and it was nice to chat about football, the way we always do. Craig and I anyway. In fact I apologise to Kate here and now for the amount of football talk that afternoon. Sorry, Kate!

When I returned to Tower Bridge the next day I felt a little odd. It was a strange sensation to think that this was to be my last day on the River Thames, all being well. I was only thirteen miles or so from the Thames Barrier and success. Suddenly I didn't want this edventure to end, so I had got back to the finish/start line a little earlier to take it all in and reflect on what I was presumably about to finish. I sat on the south bank watching the boats go past, the tourists marvelling at HMS *Belfast*, County Hall and Tower Bridge. Most of all I marvelled myself at the fantastic Tower of London. It always blows me away when I look at the White Tower and consider that it has probably been there since the year 1100. Flipping heck, that is a whole lot of history! It has seen so much, I am tempted to say everything; all the legendary Kings and Queens, the prisoners, executions, the world changing around it. It even housed the London Olympic 2012 medals! I am lucky enough to have travelled a bit but I can honestly say that I love the Tower of London more than almost anywhere else in the world. Fantastic – and I only wish that time travel was possible because, if it was, one of the things I would do is to go back and have a look at The Tower over the years. That said, I'd be very careful to not mix in the wrong crowds – it is all very well loving that place but I think I'd have had considerably different feelings about it if I had ever been a prisoner there.

I had allowed myself to get distracted and had to get moving. I jumped off the wall that I was sitting on, winced because such an action hurt my leg again, put my backpack on, re-tied my shoelaces and, for the last time, and perhaps a little theatrically, headed off to the Thames Barrier. Except that, all the other times, I had been heading to a stopping point on my way to it but this time I was quite literally running to the finish line. It was a very reflective run; most of my thoughts during this leg of the journey focused on what had come before. I thought back to the people I had met, the places I had seen, the feelings I had felt and my, by now, much better leg injury. It was a strange one that, it seemed as though I had basically just run it off. Maybe it was simply a case of my body adjusting to the daily grind and adapting to this silliness. Whatever the reason, I was now able to run more freely and so I did.

Again I thought about all the years that I had felt I would never do anything special and with every step a load lifted from my shoulders. I had always lived under the belief that I was a bit of a nobody, a nice enough bloke but one that was never going to do anything noteworthy. Yet here I was on my way to achieving something that would always be with me, a very real achievement. As I ran I literally felt myself gaining some genuine self-confidence and you know what? It felt great. I realised that I was not a loser after all and it felt like the sun came out from behind a bloody massive cloud. I had beaten my demons.

Brilliantly this part of the Thames Path is mostly by the river and I plodded along the south bank past Bermondsey and Rotherhithe then past the Surrey Docks City Farm which amused me because it had a massive model cow outside. There was no-one around to take my photo with it sadly but it does seem appropriate that I saw a cow once more before I finished this run, even if it is made of plastic. After Lechlade I prefer that type anyway.

It was a strange old day. I had spent fourteen months building up to this. I had dreamt of it and had worked very hard on it. I had lived it and I had loved it, even on the days when the whole thing seemed like the impossible dream. But it wasn't impossible, I was soon to do it, job done. Job complete, I was soon to finish running the whole length of the River Thames. I knew then that I would miss it. The daily grind had become the norm for me now. Whereas I had expected to by now be desperate to get this over and done with, I felt quite the opposite. I just didn't want to stop.

Past Sayers Court Park, a quiet looking place indeed, I kept going. Apparently this was once a beautiful garden but the naughty Peter the Great, Tsar of Russia, ruined it, drunk with his mates in 1698 while staying there during his ship-building studies. Soon I could see the towers of Canary Wharf and, left foot, right foot, I spotted the domed tower of the Royal Observatory. I was surprised after that to come across a statue of that rascal Peter the Great. It had been a gift from Russia to mark the tercentenary of the Tsar's time in London. It is a nice statue, don't misunderstand me, but I couldn't help but find it a little disappointing that Peter the Great has a statue in London after studying here for a bit, during which time he and his mates smashed up what was then apparently one of England's most impressive gardens – but Sir Joseph Bazalgette re-designs London, saving lots of cholera-related deaths in the process and he doesn't get one? The thought also occurred that if London rewarded every student that has ever studied here and drunkenly vandalised something a statue then there wouldn't be any space left for anything else, which was quite a clever thought really.

I had been saddened in 2007 to hear that the *Cutty Sark* had caught fire and was very badly damaged. So I was delighted to see the famous tea clipper up ahead and can report that she is a fine sight indeed. It seemed strange to think that I would be seeing her again in a few days during the London Marathon.

I was now a mere five-and-three-quarters miles from the Thames Barrier, right on track for my scheduled arrival of 2pm and my excitement was building. I am not going to lie to you, dear reader, I was immensely proud of myself and saw no reason not to be. I was held up for a bit in front of the stunning Royal Naval College by a film crew whose representative did a fine job of politely telling me to shut up and stay still. It was a period piece of some kind so, if you ever see such a show, look in the background as there might well be a bloke dressed all in red being dragged out of shot by an increasingly exasperated lady who was surely by that time seriously starting to question her career choice. I got a bit too excited there, I just wanted to be on the telly!

Yet again, like so many times before, I found myself wanting to stop and explore. There is just so much to do in London and on the Thames. We are so lucky to have it. I actually think that we all take it for granted. It is always the same isn't it? I am convinced that my friends and family abroad have seen more of London in their short visits here than I have managed in my lifetime. Mind you, this run of mine is certainly helping me to tick things off – I have seen so much since leaving Kemble that it is quite staggering. It truly has been a labour of love, the trip of a lifetime.

I have tried to be honest throughout telling you this story and I shall be here too: In 1999, as the new millennium approached and the party people announced the erection of the Millennium Dome, I openly laughed at the idea of a "big tent" celebrating its arrival. Why, when we had buildings hundreds of years old, were we erecting something like this, that was scheduled to remain for about

40 years? And I was right too, I think. Or at least I was at that point. Today it has been sponsored and re-named the O2 Arena and is a very welcome and fabulous sight. Especially if you have, I don't know, just run the whole length of the River Thames, or at least most of it by this time.

I have seen events there and it is actually a great venue. I really like it. I ran around the outside of it, following the Thames as ever, and appreciated Ordnance Jetty which was once a pier but now transformed into a wildlife area. Environmental conservation is something that has been growing on me in recent times so I found it interesting, this recycling of land. No cows there either. The signs were all now saying "Thames Barrier" and counting down the mileage but I couldn't see it yet. It felt like I never would but then, once I passed the Greenwich Yacht Club and the London Port Health Authority, I finally set eyes, for the first time ever, on the Thames Barrier.

It was a hell of a moment. I was there and clearly nothing would stop me now. I am not ashamed in the slightest to tell you that I found this quite an emotional moment and I raised my arms to the sky several times, punching the air, laughing to myself and repeating the words "I've done it" several times.

I had run practically 184 miles and, talk about brilliant planning, I was right on time for my arrival party. This had been a great success. I had raised my fundraising total and then some too. As I prepared to round the second to last corner I looked up to the sky and blew a kiss to Grandma; "Never believe that you are a loser again, Ed," I uttered under my breath. Now let's finish what I had started. I saw Mum, Dad, Lucy, Richard and Emma as soon as I came round this corner and I started to punch the air again with both arms, a massive smile on my face as their cheers, clapping and whooping got louder and louder. Hello Thames Barrier! The last vague bend negotiated, I entered the last straight and jumped into the sky, punching it like the football player that scores the World Cup Winning

Goal in front of his own fans and then rushes to celebrate with them. Maybe this was my World Cup win, finally! The last step since Kemble carried me over the finishing line and I ran basically into a hug with Mum and Dad, which was unexpected but appropriate given all the support they had given me over the years. Lucy filmed me on her mobile, Richard on the camcorder and Emma gave me a glass of champagne. I did my interviews for Facebook and general posterity. I really felt elated and was greatly moved when they gave me a photo frame containing some photos from the start of the run all that time ago. To this day it hangs on my wall at home and it is a prized possession.

At the same time however, it did feel a little anti-climatic. I think that I had built it up so much in my head over all those months and miles that reality was always going to struggle to match up with the fantasy. I did feel great, you must understand, just not as great as I thought I would feel.

I wonder if those blokes who laughed at me from their car those times when I was out training for this exact moment had done something similar with their day.

Even the weather was playing the game for me today, waiting for me to get into Richard and Emma's car to go back to Greenwich Pier for the boat back to Embankment before deciding to chuck it down. Dad and Lucy were not so lucky however, getting drenched as they waited for Richard to drive back to pick them up. They were not so pleased when they called me to tell Richard to hurry up by my assertion that "well, at least I made it into the car and am dry". I think that, looking back, it probably wasn't the best time for that joke but there you go. I suppose that I should say that I was sympathetic to their plight but, actually, I was in such a great mood by now that I found it funny, which probably thinking about it doesn't put me in a very good light really. I enjoyed my massive chocolate biscuit while Richard went back to pick them up and I sat with Mum, chatting and letting my achievement sink in.

On the boat down to Embankment I realised that I had forgotten something – I wanted to bring a Union Flag to pose with on the stern, like Olympic athletes do, but alas not. I should have brought one with me and I regret that but anyway I was kind of lost in my own little world, staring at the Thames, not really thinking as such, just looking at it, like my recurring dream all that time ago.

I had vowed to not go home until the whole project was complete and of course I still had the Virgin London Marathon to go, so I stayed at Mum and Dad's where I had a couple of beers and a massive fish and chips meal by way of celebration. This was one of the best days of my life and I really wanted to celebrate but I knew that I couldn't, not totally. I had to rest up, recover well and get myself ready to go again on Sunday. I slept very well that night, as I recall.

The next two days were spent sleeping and generally resting up, trying to recharge the old batteries. Coach (brother) Richard would not allow me to do nothing so I swam a couple of times, nothing more than 20 lengths, nice and easy. I stayed off my feet and then, as marathon day approached, I began to re-focus on what was ahead of me. This was helped by a couple of local newspaper interviews that I gave where I was forced to think about what I had already achieved and what I still had to do. You can guess what I ate – carbohydrates, carbohydrates and carbohydrates. I ate carbohydrates until I was sick of the sight of 'em. Mind you I also had a super excuse to not do anything and to be really lazy for a little bit which was a strange feeling but very welcome too.

THE FINAL CHALLENGE AND BEING QUIET FOR A MINUTE, OK, MAKE THAT TWO LAST CHALLENGES

London Marathon day 2013 arrived at last and by this time, refreshed and focused, I was ready to go. It had been a sombre week in the marathon world after the bomb attacks on the Boston Marathon. The world had been rightly outraged by these events and London was putting on a show of solidarity. As runners, we were invited to show our support for the victims by wearing a black ribbon, something I was happy and proud to do. Any nerves I had were put firmly and sharply back into context with the knowledge and realisation that, no matter how I ended up feeling in the next few hours, it was not going to be as bad.

In the newspaper interviews I had given since finishing the Thames, I had been asked if I had considered pulling out of the London Marathon as a result of the Boston attacks. I replied with a firm "no". No way. If I pull out of doing something that I really want to do just because the bad guys might get me, well, they win don't they? I really think that I am right here. If I just carry on with my life then, sure, I accept that one day I might be a victim of a terrorist attack but I still think that I will have won in a way, because they didn't scare me enough to stop me living my life. Don't get me wrong, I am an absolute coward most of the time and I am mature enough to admit it both to myself and you, but I refuse to give in to these people. If they get me, they get me, but I will not stop living my life on the off chance.

I had also spent my time on the sofa wisely by making sure that I replied to the messages I had received on the edventure Facebook page and telling everyone how to track my progress via the official Virgin London Marathon website. It meant that people would hopefully be able to share in experiencing the run with me in real time.

I made my way into Greenwich Park in that there London, and mingled with other runners. I was fortunate to get to the toilets before the massive queues built up so I was able to do my business with no trouble, always one of the biggest potential troubles on a large marathon event. I then got chatting to a chap outside who was about to run and seemed like the most scared man alive. He was telling me that he had a bad stomach upset and couldn't stray too far from a toilet and did I think he would be able to get round the course? It was a bit of a difficult one to answer really because the chances were that he probably wouldn't but I didn't know how to tell him that so I just took the "well, it is going to be tough out there for you, mate" line. Basically I wimped out but I hope he managed to finish. I never saw him again after he legged it to join a massive queue for the toilet. I remember not fancying his chances though.

I popped by the British Heart Foundation base and had a spot of breakfast, consisting of a banana and bagel. After a lot of encouragement and more than a few high fives, I went and waited for what felt like hours in the pen consisting of the runners expected to finish in a time similar to mine. Here I tried to take the opportunity to chat to a few lady runners about the run ahead. Cunningly I figured that if I could manage to fit in what I had been up to these past few weeks I might get a phone number or two and Bob's your uncle. It could have been a brilliant plan and you can imagine the wedding speeches. You know how it is, it would probably make the papers, "local man marries girl after running the length of the River Thames and then meeting her at the Virgin London Marathon". The scene was all set. But I had forgotten one crucial thing; my complete and utter inability to chat women up. It has been something of a joke between me and my friends for years. So, instead of confidently approaching the ladies and saying hello, I resorted to just standing there, feeling awkward and not really speaking with anyone. In the end I just made out that I was focusing on the race the way the top runners do. I truly am that 11-year-old awkward boy who never grew up. Communication as to how I am feeling about something has always been a weakness of mine. I can think of a couple of girls who would back that up without a second thought. I always joke that I am absolutely able to speak with anyone unless I want to sleep with them.

The minute's silence for the Boston victims was very well respected and silence reigned. I found it a very emotional moment to be honest. There is something about total silence at such a large event with so many people present that I always find moving. At football matches, the minute's silence has often been replaced by a minute's applause. I don't like that as much although it is still a very nice gesture. Most people I have spoken to say it has been replaced at such an event because football fans have been occasionally known to shout during minute silences. Certainly I have seen and heard football fans making noise on purpose at such times and it greatly saddens me. Anyway, the silence here was impeccable and we were soon on our way to the start line.

There it was. The start line was now right ahead, yards ahead of me. I crossed it and instantly felt a very nasty twinge in my troublesome left thigh, just to remind me that it was still injured. I had had a very deep sports massage on it since finishing the Thames and there was no doubt it was greatly improved but I now found myself worrying that maybe it wasn't strong enough to last. To distract myself I ran the first couple of miles with a Stormtrooper. I really wish that I had carried my camera phone with me. If I ever do London again, I will do. I am convinced that I would get some cracking photos. Or one of those head video cameras. That might be fun too. Anyway, said Stormtrooper said that surprisingly the costume wasn't heavy as such. Oh no, the real problem already was the dreaded chafing, the curse of many a long-distance runner.

He pulled over after a bit too, as he wanted to "sort out this bloody chafing". He must have been in a right old state later in the race.

I love *Star Wars* and would like to run a marathon in fancy dress one day. The main reason for this is not what you would expect. Can you imagine how funny it would be to be dressed as a Stormtrooper for example on a training run? I would love that. I have this great vision of someone walking down a path in my local park one morning and then suddenly seeing a Stormtrooper or Darth Vader emerging from the forest in front of them. I think I'd really enjoy the training block on that marathon.

There is so much colour and noise at the Virgin London Marathon and it creates a pretty amazing experience for runners and spectators alike. It really helps to keep the runner motivated and relaxed and I really enjoy how the crowds come out on the day to cheer everyone on. And not just the elite runners either; oh no, the people who take substantially more time to run the course get just as much respect off the people watching as the person that wins the race, perhaps more. Next time you are in London on marathon day, or any large running event, just take a look at the crowds. They don't go home once the top athletes have gone by and that is because they are amongst the best sport fans in the world. Right up there with any other city, London Marathon day shows London in all its finest glory, just like during the 2012 Olympics where our capital really outdid itself and people even spoke to one another on the tube. If you miss the spirit of those games, just get over to London for the next marathon. You'll see it in buckets.

And there was such a massive crowd that day too! It felt like millions of people were out on the streets and that each and every one of them was desperate to see us all cross the finish line. I high-fived, bantered, was given sweets. Hell, I was even given a shot of London Ale at one point. I mean no reflection at all on the quality of that beer – I have drunk it many times previously and always enjoyed it, but at that point, after several miles running

102

already, it was one of the worst drinks I have ever had. It sounds all macho and brilliant as a beer fan to say "yeah, OK, I'll drink a beer as I run a marathon" but, speaking personally, it is an awful idea and an idea not worth doing again. That said, I did it once before when running the Chicago Marathon in 2005, when I was offered and accepted a shot of a local beer towards the end and was nearly sick, so you would think I would have learnt my lesson by now. Actually I once took a call from a relative during the Beachey Head Marathon at about the 20-mile stage I think it was. He was over from Canada and asked what I was up to: "oh just running a marathon" was my casual reply. I enjoyed his reaction, I think he thought I was joking but, no, I was soon to run up the Seven Sisters. "I always wanted to say that!" said yours truly as I hung up. The runners around me all appreciated the surreal nature of the phone call and it made me chuckle to myself for a few miles.

Back to the present and it crossed my mind more than once as to why so many people were out supporting the runners and event. To this day I still suspect that it was the famous London stubbornness. Exactly a week before the Boston Marathon had been attacked by some very nasty people with clearly very twisted minds indeed. The preceding seven days before we started our challenge was rightly taken up with shock, condemnation, grieving and a nasty sense that it could happen again here too. As I said earlier, I never contemplated pulling out but I could understand why people might. I got the impression that so many people came out to watch that day to defy these idiots that think they can scare us into submission. It reminded me of a story a Policeman once told me following an IRA bomb alert in London and a road was sealed off. As the Policeman tried to stop an older gentleman from walking past him, he explained what had happened and why he was not allowed to continue; the old man simply replied, "Hitler couldn't stop me going for a pint, nor will the IRA." Obviously he didn't get down the road on this occasion but the spirit is the same. Also look at the day after the 7th July attacks on London in 2005. I am led to believe that the tube was actually very busy the next day, despite people being told in numerous cases to work at home or elsewhere. London today refuses to submit, just like during the Blitz during the Second World War. It is a very stubborn city and today I was proud to run amongst its people again.

Tower Bridge, my favourite bridge in the world, is another sight and sound to behold on marathon day. The noise coming from the people on there is electric. When people tell me that they are going to run London I always tell them to make sure they slow down at this point and remove any headphones etc. that they might be listening to because it is something to behold. One person I gave this advice to reported back afterwards and said that the level of support and noise almost made her cry. It is that special. Practising what I preach, I slowed down here and took it all in, just jogging along. I don't know many more times I will run London and, if this is the last time, I want to remember it. So I slowed right down and took what felt like an age to cross. I also had a curious thought that the bridge would open and I would fall into the River Thames but thankfully that didn't happen, which I was quite pleased about.

This is practically the half way point which I always find a big psychological moment. That first step over the half way point means that you now have less to go than you have already done which sounds obvious and in fact is, but it is a comforting thought in the middle of running 26.2 miles 385 yards, I can assure you. But I kept on running and high-fiving; I am sure that I must have set a new world record that day. That would be exciting, I have always wanted to be a record breaker, ever since the television show I used to watch as a child. If I am honest I watched it when I was older than a child too. I have always loved the idea of people really pushing themselves to the limit and possibly beyond to achieve something.

Sometimes it is a daft idea on the surface of it but I always think that is great and we should all do something daft once in a while.

My leg was holding up quite nicely at the moment, thank you very much. I was not really pushing myself very hard at all in terms of pace and I really was not that bothered about my time. I wasn't even wearing a stop watch. This whole project had been about finishing, not running fast. I had seen some great stuff and experienced some brilliant things this past fortnight and this truly was the icing on the cake. I was absolutely loving it. At mile 16 I heard my mum, above all the noise of everyone out there on the course shout to me that I had now run 200 miles since my first tentative, nervous step in that Gloucestershire field almost two weeks ago. She sounded very proud. That put an even bigger smile on my face and a little swagger into my running. As we ran around the fantastic Tower of London to move into the last five miles or so, the thought struck that in a way my life would never be the same again. I know that sounds a bit over the top and possibly even a little arrogant but I don't mean that I expected to be interviewed on all the top television shows, knighted and cheered by thousands. What I mean by that is that I knew I had gained something that could never be taken away and something that would live with me forever. I was very close now to finishing this whole silly run, something that plenty of people told me they suspected I would never be able to do, mainly because of my injured toe from that road accident. I was proving that I had heart and that I had the drive to do something. And boy was I doing it.

Naturally I hit the dreaded wall at about mile 22, right on par for me really, and it didn't come as a surprise. I always feel like I am running well until that point in a marathon, by my standards at least. Seeing as this was my 8th marathon though, I knew what to do – I took on board an energy gel and slowed the pace down in an attempt to run through it, and in time I was feeling better and able to really take in the end of a marvellous edventure. And there suddenly was Big Ben, our old friend, who I had seen just a few days before, chiming its way to yet another milestone. If only the walls on that building could talk eh? I'd be freaked out by a talking wall, for sure, but once I got used to it, I would stop and have a listen. It would have some amazing stories.

The crowds are probably 10 deep as you turn right and enter Parliament Square. This is a spectacular feeling as you know the chances are you are a merely minutes away from completing what you set out to do. I lost myself here, I admit, and was running with such a massive smile on my face, the sort of smile that says "yes, I am gonna do it!" but I didn't stop there and actually kept shouting "yes, I am gonna do it" to the crowds as they cheered and high-fived all of us runners home. And then, the most beautiful sight of all; as I rounded the last bend, I saw the grandstand where I knew my friends Craig and Kate would probably be and, a little beyond them, I saw a line, the sort of line that I really wanted to see, the sort of line that had "FINISH" written above it in massive letters. Hello London!

Now, I am a bloke and blokes stereotypically are not supposed to admit to these sort of things but I confess to you here and now, dear reader, that I also found this to be rather an emotional moment. The job was done, how I was running now didn't matter anymore, I just had to keep moving forwards and just enjoy what was quite an incredible moment, so I raised my arms up and pointed an index finger on either hand to the Heavens. I admit it, I did what the real athletes do; I didn't whisper, I looked up beyond where my fingers were pointing and said quite loudly a little something to someone special, someone who would have been so very proud and someone that I would have loved to have got to know.

"Yo Grandma! I did it!"

AFTER THE FINISH LINE

I had such a smile on my face that you would never have believed I had just run 210.2 miles 385 yards (and climbed a tree) to get here. I collected my medal and had it hung around my neck by one of the very many brilliant volunteers that the Virgin London Marathon are famous for. After collecting my goody bag I headed to the baggage collection point where my gear was waiting. I had one last surprise for everyone – Hungdrawn Vinyls had printed me a red T-shirt (naturally, I was safe here, there are no cows in the middle of London) with the words "Yo Grandma! I did it!" printed on the front. I changed into this now and, still wearing my medal, walked off to collection point V where my mum and sister Lucy were waiting. They really liked the shirt! Hugs all round and celebratory photos taken for posterity. As we were walking to The Globe pub in Covent Garden, the age-old London Marathon tradition was very much in force – if you wear your finishers medal out on said day you will be congratulated by passers-by, people across the street, everyone wants to say well done. This was very nice for me but a nice effect was that Mum went a little crazy telling everyone she could how I hadn't "just" run a marathon but the whole length of the Thames too. It is always nice to make your parents proud, kids. So it was a very enjoyable walk and a tremendous feeling mentally as I received lots of very nice comments, but I really wanted to sit down and was grateful that I had had the foresight to reserve some seating for everyone who was in town that had come to support me as my feet were now blistered and bloody killing me. It felt like beer o'clock.

One of the most beautiful moments in my life occurred as I walked through the front door of The Globe pub, as all my supporters present clapped me and cheered! For a few seconds even people I didn't know were clapping and I milked it a little by smiling, punching the air, kissing my medal and then opening my arms like a rock star on stage as if to give everyone a hug. That was a tremendous moment and it got better as people came over to shake my hand and say well done. Forget everything else, this was my moment in time. I will never forget that minute or so for as long as I live.

And it wasn't just in person that people were congratulating me either. When I eventually logged onto the edventure Facebook page I saw that lots of people had indeed being following my marathon run, right from the minute I crossed the start line. All of them saying "come on Ed" or "Ed is now half way through". It was almost as if they were commentating on my run! And, when it was announced that I had officially crossed the finish line and I had obviously achieved all I set out to do and then some, the comments changed to a very congratulatory nature, with people saying all kinds of nice things about me. So many great memories to look back on from all this when I am an old man.

I sat down finally and had quite a few beers, relaxed and taking in what I had achieved, catching up with friends and family. My dad and Aunt Vicky were pretty surprised and grateful when I pointed out my T-shirt. Grandma had passed away a very long time ago now but here, today, she was back in the room in a way and it felt right to remember her here in her own capital city. So I did something that I always wanted to do, ever since I started all this. I put up a status on the Facebook page which said "I want to tell you something I haven't said before. This whole project is dedicated to Grandma Vanson". It just seemed the right time to do something like this and I received plenty of comments and "likes" from people. Some even said that she would be proud. My dad echoed that thought later on as we walked to the station and these sentiments made me feel very proud and to be honest a little choked up for a moment, although the beer may have had something to do with that. During the course of the afternoon in the pub I had noticed that someone had a balloon with the words "go Ed" written on it and I walked back to Waterloo Station with it tied to my backpack before returning to my parents' house and drinking more booze with my sister, celebrating an unlikely success. What a day. What a bloody day.

THE DAY AFTER THE FINISH LINE AND BEYOND

Everything for the past fortnight had been generally regulated time-wise, as I had had to use as much of the daylight hours as possible and had to sleep as much as possible to aid my recovery from the day's exertions. As a result I was in a real maverick mood when I awoke late. I had gone to bed in the early hours as was always my intention. No matter how tired I was I would never have gone to bed before midnight – it had been one of the most special days of my life and I was not going to waste a minute of it. No way, I had to live the day in full and that I did.

When I eventually rolled over and sat on the edge of the bed in my parents' spare bedroom, the emotions of the day before ran through my mind quickly. It all seemed a little unreal, like it hadn't really happened. But there, on the bedside cabinet was my official Virgin London Marathon Finishers Medal. It had not been a dream after all. I showered, changed and went down for breakfast. Everybody bar Dad was at work so we sat and chatted for a bit. It was all very nice but really I felt a little strange. More than anything I really just wanted to shout from the rooftops what I had just done and I felt a little annoyed at the world for moving on so fast. I realised that already the achievement was in the past now. Less than 24 hours after my ambition was realised and I was already feeling a little flat, not to mention restless. There was only one thing for it. So I went out and ran 26 miles.

Get out of it, I am only joking. I did not see my running shoes for ages after the marathon and I didn't come close to running anything at all that day. I didn't even consider it. I put on some music and started to write some notes which form the basis of this book instead.

I have heard stories before of real athletes who reach a high and realise their dream before experiencing a real down right after. I guess it was inevitable, but for a couple of weeks after it was all a bit flat. I mean, I had felt on top of the world but was brought to earth by the return to work and the real world. I was constantly thinking of what challenge was next and what had been before. For example, one of my great unfulfilled ambitions is to complete a full pull-up in the gym. I kid you not, I have never been able to do it so that is one thing I will get to work on. On a larger scale, I have a few ideas for future challenges, both personal ones and ones where I think I can possibly raise a few bob for charity but I'll keep them to myself for now. You'll hear about them soon enough. Maybe there will be another book in it!

I have really enjoyed telling you this story and hope you have enjoyed it too. You will have guessed that I really did love the run, despite the injured leg, and consider it one of the finest achievements, probably, that I will ever manage. The whole being chased by cows bit is true, I promise, and that was possibly the funniest bit of the whole fortnight. I think that I developed within myself over this project – but what have I learnt? Well, firstly I have discovered a new layer to myself –I am not such a loser that I am destined to do nothing with my life and certainly it is true that I now see a potential within myself to complete challenges such as this. I think that I have also realised again that the world is beautiful and I want to do as much as I possibly can with my limited time on the planet.

This whole run has also given me time to think and I really think this whole achievement has given me the confidence to believe that I can make some kind of small difference to the world. As a consequence I would like to do some more fundraising. I don't know for whom yet, and I don't know when either. What I do is know that I need a bit of a break mentally as it has been tough and all-encompassing. When I have had a chance to clear my head and rest up a bit I will get back to it, one way or the other. I like to keep busy and suspect that I would like to get involved in volunteering too, in an attempt to put something back into a world that has already given me so much. I had one big thought that I would like to share with you now. It occurred to me whilst I was out on the Thames in a remote field, the sort of field that I cannot actually remember where it is. My thought is as follows, it is a pretty simple one really: If we all try and make the world a better place; if we all do the right thing and be nice to the people we meet, the world will become a better place won't it? I know that I will try to do exactly that in terms of the charity work and fundraising I do and in the way I conduct myself.

I like to write and have always wanted to write a book but never got around to it. I have now finally finished my first book and you have just finished reading it.

Peace and Love,
Ed Vanson
Epsom

EDVENTURE RUNNING

FURTHER POINTS

✓   I raised a final total of £5829.08 (including gift aid).

✓   Which makes me feel all warm and fuzzy inside.

✓   My toenail fell off shortly after the Virgin London Marathon. Photographic evidence is available if needed.

✓   I am now an uncle to a little girl. Her parents have already taken me aside and made me promise to "not put stupid thoughts in her head about running silly distances" when she is older. However I am still looking forward to telling her this story and hopefully taking her for a jog one day. Maybe I'll take her to the Thames when I do so and let her make her own mind up.

✓   My friends Craig and Kate were indeed in the grandstand as I finished the marathon itself and I am not embarrassed at all to say that I gave them both a hug when we met up in the pub.

✓   I was twice asked by the British Heart Foundation to address the people on their 2014 Virgin London Marathon team and tell them what I had done and how I had raised the money, giving them tips and encouragement. I hope it was of use to them. I really enjoyed it and even had them high-fiving each other at one point in my presentation. It just seemed the right thing to do as I love a high five. I suspect that I possibly went a bit Alan Partridge or David Brent and it was at this point during one of the presentations I heard one man in the audience refer to me as "bizarre".

✓   When walking back from the work canteen to my desk on a particularly hot day shortly after returning to work, someone actually did stop me and ask if I was Ed Vanson and then about the Thames run. I felt famous for 5 seconds.

✓ A friend suggested that I called this book *50 shades of Ed* but I prefer this title.

✓ I have still not decided on which actor could play me in the Hollywood version of this story. Any suggestions would be gratefully received so long as it is neither "Sloth" nor "Shrek" thank you very much. During the course of writing this book, however, I found a website that asks you questions and works out who would play you in a story of your life. This has been a particular point of mystery throughout this story and I am pleased to say that this scientific brilliance resulted in an answer of esteemed actor Benedict Cumberbatch. Not someone I would have thought of by myself but you can't argue with an online search engine as we all know, so once this book is commissioned as a film I will try and find a way to contact him and offer him the gig.

✓ I also still need a narrator for the spoken book. Ideally someone with a better, more easy-on-the-ear voice than mine. Feel free to offer your services if you like and we'll see what we can arrange.

✓ In March 2016 Fulham Football Club announced that they intend to erect and subsequently place a George Cohen statue at their Craven Cottage home and establish a George Cohen legacy, helping various local dementia charities through fundraising and awareness.

✓ A short while after I finished this project I wrote to Thames Water and asked if they would consider a more prominent Sir Joseph Bazalgette memorial. I am delighted to report that I heard back very promptly and actually when the new sewer is constructed and working, there will be a new memorial of some kind celebrating his contribution to London and the incredible life he led. This is currently due in the year 2020. Again I think this is brilliant and I fully support that too, for what it's worth.

✓ A couple of days after the Virgin London Marathon I went to Grandma's grave, laid some flowers and told her what I had been up to. I like to think she was pretty stoked.

✓ I may well be fat but at least I did something better and more constructive than just shouting abuse at passing strangers. Easy to shout from a car isn't it, lads?

The story I have just told you is all totally true and I put in a lot of hard work to make it happen. It is only right however that I acknowledge with grateful thanks the work of so many people, without whom everything you have just read could probably never have been successful.

So a big thank you in alphabetical order to Aldabella (Epsom), Alroy, Aunt Vicky, British Heart Foundation, Cat, Ceri, Chloe, Claire-Marie, Craig, Dad, Daisy, Dan, Darrell, Dave, Ed the Pub Landlord, Emma, Hungdrawn Vinyl (Ewell), Jade, James, Kate, Kerrie, Lesley, Linda, Lorraine, Lucy, Mum, Natalie, Nick, Nicky, Peter, Rachel, Richard, Rikki, Rosie, Run to Live (Ashtead), Rose Revived (Newbridge),Russell, Shutes Tattoos, Scwif, Sally, Sam, Steveo, The Bag Moving Volunteers, The New Inn (Lechlade), Tony, Trout and The Wild Duck Inn (Ewen).

This book is dedicated to everyone who helped me, supported me and believed in me. But in particular this book is dedicated to the memory of Grandma Vanson and Craig Ayres, both of whom, quite without knowing it, provided me with plenty of inspiration and support throughout all this.

edventurerunning@hotmail.co.uk

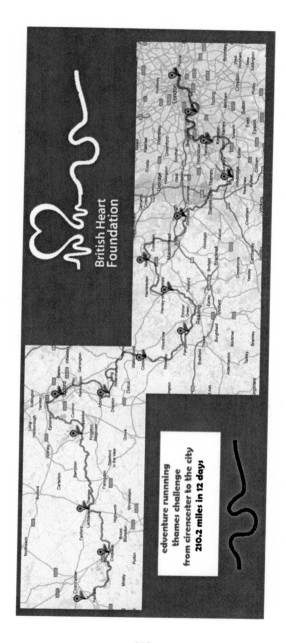

British Heart
Foundation

edventure runnning
thames challenge
from cirencester to the city
210.2 miles in 12 days

Lightning Source UK Ltd.
Milton Keynes UK
UKOW02f1422301116
288819UK00002B/34/P